Published by Lark

This edition published in the UK in 2021

Copyright © Lucy Nichol 2021

ISBN: 978-1-8383744-0-2

Cover design by enough (www.enoughdesign.co.uk)
Front cover photo: Paul 'Gigsy' McGivern
Back cover photo of 'He-Man': Paul Taylor and Christopher Mitton

Also available as an ebook edition: ISBN 978-1-8383744-1-9

THE TWENTY SEVEN CLUB

LUCY NICHOL

To all the lives behind the headlines that we cannot
truly claim to know…

PROLOGUE

April 8, 1994. The day the music died.

'Kurt Cobain found dead' screamed unapologetically from every black-inked front page landing on doormats or in front gardens around the world. Fans cried in despair, conspiracy theorists looked for someone to blame, and kids on the edge of a punk-rock love affair were at risk of returning to saccharine pop.

A tragic loss to the music world and a kick in the teeth for my jilted generation.

I'd only popped round to Dad's for a Saturday morning cuppa. A catch up on last night's Columbo. The dissection of a fictional murder enquiry with a few dodgy impressions thrown in.

I got far more than I bargained for when he broke the tragic news to me.

'Emma. That rocker you're always talking about, he's dead.'

'Rocker? What you on about, Dad?'

'He's dead. Shot himself. In the head.'

My dad, far too casually for my liking, dropped the bombshell.

To say I was gutted…

'He was your age Emma.' Dad continued, with his head still stuck in the Saturday paper and his hand seemingly stuck in a packet of KP nuts.

He wasn't.

'I'm not 27 'til December Dad.'

'Aren't you? How old are you then?'

He was never good at maths, but I think this was more a sign that he wasn't listening. He was very good at tuning in and out. I always wondered if that was a 'dad thing', or a 'my-dad thing'. I tried to clarify:

'Obviously, if I turn 27 in December, then I must be 26. Anyway, how do you not know how old your own daughter is?'

That light bit of criticism didn't really sink in either. He continued reading and scoffing dry-roasted peanuts – the coating of which was tainting the newspaper article about Kurt's final moments.

I felt as though I was intruding on a dark and private time. Kurt's final moments, full of anguish, were all over the news – and they had travelled all the way from Seattle to my little corner of Hull – marking their presence by landing in a soggy, papery mess on my dad's muddy door mat.

'Ses 'ere he was a heroin addict too. Same old sad story.'

It was true. There were too many stories with the same ending. Too many brilliant rock stars losing their fight with heroin or alcohol or sleeping pills. But perhaps their fight was actually with the darkness in their heads. Maybe the drugs were simply a precarious cushion that kept needing to be puffed up until one day it was too much and they hit the deck.

A heart attack in the bath.

A drowning in the pool.

A bullet in the head.

Kurt wasn't the first, and he probably wouldn't be the last. Janis Joplin. Jimi Hendrix. Jim Morrison. Brian Jones…all dead at 27.

'Why do so many rock stars die aged 27?' I pondered out loud, to nobody in particular.

'I've lost many an idol over the years, Emma. It's the price they pay for talent.'

'But why 27? I mean, I get it. Rock stars are rarely straight-forward creatures. But why 27? It can't be a huge coincidence surely?'

Dad just raised his eyebrows and shrugged. It seemed he had moved onto the sports pages now. He was no doubt looking to see how his beloved Tigers were doing in the league.

But I struggled with death. Whether it was someone I knew, or admired from afar, or a stranger whose final moments hit the headlines of the Hull Daily Mail, it always shook me up and reminded me just how fragile life is. I remember when comedian Tommy Cooper had a heart attack on stage when I was sixteen. Everyone in class was taking the piss, using the comedian's famous catchphrase to turn his death into a joke:

'Did you hear about Tommy Cooper. Dead. Just like that.'

'One minute he was cracking jokes, the next he was having a heart attack. Just like that.'

I just couldn't get into the joke. The idea of death set me on edge. It had the capability of engulfing me in waves of dread and darkness. It was certainly a weird contradiction, being so afraid of life's dark side, yet listening to music that talked of little else. It's like that saying - keep your friends close and your enemies closer. Maybe if I was on familiar terms with the whole idea of death it wouldn't do as much damage? Perhaps I would be prepared for it?

However, as I was now catapulting towards the year of 'do or die', with Kurt's death reminding us that an early passing at age 27 was becoming more and more plausible, I was starting to panic.

Stupidly, I dabbled with the very things that put your health at risk, simply to stop me worrying about my health – and, importantly, the health of everyone around me. I kind of felt responsible for people. Mum had an affair, so when I was little I thought I needed to step up and look after my heartbroken dad. That's what my young brain decided at the time, anyway. And regardless of who really did the looking after, I always *felt* responsible.

I remember meeting my lovely lad Trevor for the first time at the dog shelter. There was no way I could leave him there. I simply had to take him home. I had the power to stop his pain.

Responsibility is a heavy burden to carry. So I needed the occasional weekend blowouts – even though the aftermath reinforced my negative thinking patterns, I had to let off steam at some point or I'd simply blow.

But back to Kurt Cobain. He was like a strangely comforting bed of nails, like most punk rock artists I guess, but higher on the talent barometer. You find comfort in them purely because they remind you that you're not alone in your discomfort. There are two emotions fighting against each other like alcohol and cocaine. A sadness that wants to lie still and indulge in the comfort of the pain, and an edginess that wants to freak the fuck out.

I'd grown up on a diet of rock music. Mum and Dad were always going to gigs in spit 'n' sawdust pubs. Usually some local band I'd never heard of. But they also introduced me to Janis, Jimi and co at an early age and, whilst most kids thought their parents were the epitome of cringe, I was always fascinated by mine. Until Mum decided to have her affair when I was just a young kid. That monumental act laid the foundations for seriously tortured teenager. And here I am today, an adult with a full-time job, my own home, a pet whippet and a slightly out of control recreational coke habit.

Oh to be a kid again.

Back in the day, when I was a mere tot, I'd get to pick my favourite babysitter and Mum and Dad would go off into the night to drink whiskey and listen to bands. Meanwhile, I would spend the night making ice-cream sodas and watching horror films that I was blatantly far too young to watch.

I still can't get rid of the vision of that guy in the woods ripping off all his skin and muscles and turning into a werewolf. I never dared tell my parents where the source of my primary school night terrors lay (it lay squarely at the feet of my favourite babysitter whose sugar-laden drinks kept me awake and buzzing long enough to soak up all the scary shit I wasn't supposed to see).

If I didn't get my favourite babysitter, I'd offer to go up to bed early because it was better reading my Wonder Woman annual for the hundredth time than sitting with Maureen all night while she watched Dallas.

So with horror movies and punk rock I was kind of always drawn to pain and darkness. But you have to wonder which came first – the punk or the pain. The two always seemed to go hand in hand. And I'm guessing all those safety pins in the 70s didn't do much to relieve it. So all this heroin and death, well, it must have been a form of pain relief.

There was something warming about punk rock despite the pins and the pain, in a weird sort of way. Like the ache in your chest when you're about to sob your heart out and it feels oddly comforting. I think it's to do with normalising your anguish. You know, like, look, you're not on your own with feeling distressed about the fact your Dr Martens won't wear in or the fact you lost your brand-new Black Cherry lipstick. Because Kurt Cobain is pretty pissed off about being famous. He's pretty pissed off by all the pain. You're both pissed off. You're on a level.

You are not alone.

In almost every other situation, however, I definitely did feel alone.

So it's probably no surprise that by the time I got to my late teens and early twenties, I was all about The Pixies and Babes in Toyland, Nirvana and The Senseless Things. I felt kind of angry about shit. I still don't know what shit I was angry about, but I was definitely angry. And they were kind of angry about shit too. It felt, to me, like a natural progression from what my parents introduced me to.

Which is why I could never understand why Dad didn't like my music. I argued that it was today's version of Janis Joplin. Of the Stones. But he wasn't convinced.

'Screaming like you've swallowed a box of nails and speaking in tongues is just not poetic, Emma.'

It was a dark April day when the news about Kurt Cobain's suicide hit. The rain was heaving down on Dad's budding Californian Lilac - the only plant left thriving in his little backyard. I often sat by the window, drinking a strong cup of tea whilst looking at the plant's transformation as the days and weeks ticked by. The buds slowly turned from a warm dusky pink to a cooler purple before they burst open as tiny blue petals. Like floral pompoms erupting from dark green stems and reminding us that the tired looking evergreen had passion in it yet.

As I marvelled at the buds beginning to make their annual breakthrough, I spied Trevor lifting his skinny little leg and aiming a powerful, steaming jet of yellow liquid at the delicate little flowers.

'That bloody dog's pissing on your mum's Californian Lilac again, Emma.'

Although Mum had moved on years ago, Dad still insisted it was her plant. He wasn't much of a gardener generally, but that plant was mulched and fed and pruned to within an inch of its life. Weird how 'Mum's' plant stood out in all its beauty against the backdrop of a flailing Buddleia and a yellowing Holly, when my memory serves up images of her in a very different light.

Dad seemed to be in denial about the way my mum had behaved.

I opened the back door and called Trevor in. His ears pricked up and he looked over at me – I swear that dog can smile. He came galloping towards me with his tongue hanging out. Of course, given the weather, he continued to cause chaos by running straight into the kitchen dripping wet and muddy. Dad shook his head and grabbed the nearest tea-towel to scrub the dirty carpet tiles with. It made it worse.

'Bloody dog' he muttered. I don't think he wanted Trevor to hear his insults. He loved him really. I know this because I could often hear Dad talking to Trev as if he were another offspring. It just appeared to be a bit of a Marmite relationship between the two of them.

Kind of like punk rock.

'Some say they'd signed a deal with the Devil to give themselves genius talent', Dad said of our missing rock stars, suddenly jumping back into the subject. I guessed the football news couldn't have been good.

'Don't be ridiculous, Dad. That's a load of old shite that.'

This is the problem, you see, with the media. It becomes all about conspiracy theories and Satanists when there's obviously a real and raw reason why 27 is the age that some of us expire. There were no deals with the devil. But there had to be a reason.

'There was this one guy', Dad said as he wiped the sticky dry roasted peanut dust off his fingers and onto a clean tea-towel, 'who, legend has it, couldn't play guitar at all one minute, and the next was like some kind of Eric Clapton. A genius of the strings. A finger-picking prodigy. It had to be the work of the Devil.'

And so talent, he suggested, carried a high price; because no sooner had the miracle guitarist showcased his tremendous plucking talent to the world...

'...he was dead.' Dad finished.

CHAPTER 1

'You heard the news, Dave? Wanna get wasted down The Angel?'

My heavy heart was worthy of sixth form poetry. It needed indulging. And, much as he was often more concerned about the Gallagher Brothers in Manchester than Kurt and co in Washington, it didn't take much to convince Dave that we needed a night of intoxication.

Of course, I knew it was time to leave when we started lighting up the Drambuie. Experience tells me that it only takes one Drambuie-fuelled stumble to the bar to move onto the harder stuff. But I don't listen to experience. Who does?

Drambuie is a fitting beverage for The Angel though, with its sweet mince-pie festive aroma. All warm and cosy, familiar but with a bit of an edge and a feeling that, even though you've been there a thousand times before, anything could happen. As the warming mince pie sensation hits your throat it lights a fuse that sends a smattering of fireworks to your now completely alive and excitable brain.

And then what does your brain do? Decide to move away from the warmth and excitability and into the Tequila zone. Sorry, the Tequila and Diamond White zone (explainer - you need a longer drink accompaniment to reduce the number of return trips to the bar).

Oh Tequila. Why do you always wink at me so?

There were some students slamming Tequilas in the Angel a few weeks previous. One of them, who reminded me a little of Dylan the Rabbit from the Magic Roundabout, complete with standard-issue beige corduroy flares and a better fringe than I had in the 70s, knocked his shot straight back like a boss. Then, as his head came forward again, puked it straight back up onto the carpet, along with a recently ingested curry from Ray's Place.

Poor lad.

I swear the Mexican beverage is the main reason stiletto heels stick to pub carpets. Even for the most accomplished slammer it lingers in the throat with vom-threatening vibes, pulsating in an involuntary rhythm, until... bleeeeuuurrrgggghhhh!

Still, if I was going to drink Tequila anywhere, remaining in the safety of the Angel was the smartest move that one could make.

My home from home, The Angel has that old-school real-pub-comfort vibe about it. The furniture is high-quality real wood, covered with high-quality real leather, and carpeted with a high-quality Axminster (albeit one that gets a regular spattering of booze and undigested Indian food).

However, the décor, nice as it is, as it was, is all older than me now – it's knackered, dented and ripped.

The punters are very much a part of the furniture. There's rarely any surprise about who you might bump into. The only thing that really changes is the influx of as-yet-untainted fresher's students each September - and they only visit briefly to score marijuana from the bucket-hat-clad friendly dealer, quickly downing a pint of lager before moving on to their student union bar for social safety. Weed is generally a major part of any university initiation ceremony. Hence, the pot-induced 'whitey' plays a major role in fresher's week too. Another reason the Axminster enjoys a regular spattering.

Bob and Brenda have presided over the Angel for as long as anyone can remember. They've never had kids, so obviously decided to satisfy their parental instincts by dealing with a bunch of 'kidults' in a Hull pub. They're like those teachers you secretly respected at school. You give them grief but you never overstep the mark because, as much as they're looking after you, you're ever so slightly scared of them. This is because 1) they're distant relatives of the most infamous family in Hull and 2) where the fuck else would we go on a Friday night?

Away from the bar, hiding in the shadows, you've got the two older guys who visit daily, drink Old Peculiar, read broadsheet newspapers and never speak. Not to each other, not to anyone. They both sport long thinning grey hair and long raincoats and always sit in the same adjacent seats by the wall. They look like brothers from another mother, and yet not a word is uttered – not even to Bob and Brenda, who know exactly what they want because it hasn't changed in over a decade (a steady stream of Old Peculiar, culminating in a single malt whiskey before they both leave around 10pm.)

I wonder where they go?

Then there's Doreen – the life and soul whose permanent seat at the bar is touched by nobody else. Ever. Doreen is The Angel's angel. Those students think they're living it up but nobody can out-party Doreen. She's always there for the lock-ins, raising a glass with a smile and a cheeky wink to Dave. I hope I carry that kind of charm and energy when I hit my 70s. Shit, I barely carry any of it now. Maybe we acquire charm as we age?

The Angel is Doreen's lifeline, the centre of her world. She's always on the guest list for Christmas dinner with Bob and Brenda and I rarely see her paying for her half pints of milk stout. A real part of the family.

And then there's Dave. My best mate Dave. We always position ourselves at a little round table on little round stools, just close enough to the bar to yell our orders to Bob and Brenda. Dave's been there for-seemingly-ever and he's an interesting source of conversation and random facts. I've witnessed him passionately educating the pub on the origins of weevils in flour, the plight of Hull's former fishermen and, as per when the Drambuie starts attacking Dave's brain cells, turning nouns into verbs.

'Take me to your sleepery and lose me forever'

Ironically, he was asleep just moments after delivering that tempting proposition to the poor woman who was, unfortunately for her, sharing our bar table a few weeks ago. I say sharing, she was perched on the end leaning clearly away from us with a tilt that would almost certainly topple the Tower of Pisa. So Dave wasn't sleeping in her sleepery after all. He was snoring in the subsequently derelict drinkery, beneath a sittery in dire need of a pissery.

Prick. Don't think I've seen the poor woman in here since then.

Anyway, tonight wasn't going to be much different. I was indulging in darkness.

'Why'd he do it, Dave?' I wailed into my pint of lager. 'Why'd he feel he had no other choice?'

'Kurt wanted out Emma. Who wouldn't? Just look at the state of the world today. The Tories are in power for fuck's sake. Fancy a line?'

'He's American Dave. The Tories won't have had much impact. Ah yeah, go on then.'

I hotfooted it to the loos with Dave's little bag of powder tucked safely in my back pocket. The lovely Angel loos still hadn't been refurbished and yet I was about to inhale a concoction of toilet germs, cocaine and God knows what else mixed in with it all from the cistern.

I didn't care though. Tonight, I had good reason. And I could feel the excitement even before I placed a little of the white powder on the top of the cistern. I took out my bank card and expertly created a nice, neat little line. Just a little one. Just enough for tonight. I could feel my heart pounding as I rolled up a note. A familiar sense of ease and joy. Something to soften the angst and anxiety.

The sound of air and powder being forced up deep into my eager nostril was bliss. I took another sniff to make

sure it was all staying in place. Shook my head a little. Felt
the satisfying bitter trickle down the back of my throat.
And walked back out as if nothing had happened. Well,
trying to look as if nothing had happened.

'Another Tequila, Dave?'

'Aye, go on then'

We were off. Talking at a thousand miles an hour.
Feeling like the kids in school who dished it all out and
never got a peep of bother back. We were the fucking
business.

I ordered the Tequilas.

'Steady on, Emma.' Brenda said, taking my money for
the toxic beverage all the same. 'You two on a mission
tonight?'

'Yup, Bren. Haven't you heard? We've lost one of our
generation's most important spokespeople.'

'John Prescott's dead?'

Was it even worth explaining who Kurt Cobain is – was
– to someone who thought an East Hull Labour MP was
the spokesperson for generation X?

'No, Bren. A musician. An artist. We're gutted. We
deserve Tequila.'

'Yeah and the rest. You know it does you no good the
morning after. I don't want to see you in here at 11am
panicking about your racing heart again.'

I defiantly necked the Tequila, then headed back to our
table, dropping Dave's into his waiting hand. He drained it
in an instant.

'Another beer, Emma?'

'Why not, mate'.

Dave returned to the little round table with two pints
and a couple of bottles of strong Diamond White cider,
'for old time's sake'. Of course, given the cocaine, I was
more than confident I could manage a couple more drinks.

I wasn't as confident about my future, however. 'I'm not
sure I'm going to make it to my 28th birthday.'

'Sorry, Emma, but you're hardly Courtney Love. I don't think you're likely to be the next one inducted into the rock 'n' roll hall of fame before keeling over on stage for the entire population of the world's teenagers to mourn over.'

It was true. I was certainly no rock star. But I can play guitar. And I'm fairly good at it. The voice leaves a lot to be desired, but you can't have everything. Unless you strike a deal with the Devil, according to my father.

Or maybe I should have just swallowed a packet of rusty nails.

I was always jealous of women who could scream like Courtney Love or Kat Bjelland, the lead singer of one of my favourite bands, Babes in Toyland. But no amount of chain-smoking Marlboro Reds was going to give me the voice of a cool-as-fuck rock star. I tried though. Which was pretty antisocial of me given that I lived in a terraced house.

So famous I am not. But I still had my age and an immense love of rock n roll in common with the tragically deceased. I was brought up on a diet of it. And they say you are what you eat. So I'm really not convinced I will make it to 28. Not if they all haven't. Life is always on a cliff edge. Every time you cross the road. Every time you take a flight. Every time you snort a line of cocaine.

I quickly shook that thought away.

There was a local lad in a band who passed away the other year. He was definitely in his 20s when he was electrocuted by his own guitar while playing in some dive pub in town.

Apparently, the crowd were really going for it then, bam, he was on the floor. At first, they thought it was some kind of stage trick. But of course, the pub in question didn't have any special effects that could do that kind of trickery. What they did have, though, was a leaky roof and dodgy cabling.

Still, it was quite a legendary way to go. I wonder if he'll be remembered like the others.

'Another line, Dave?'

The idea of cocaine being bad for you is null and void when you're high on cocaine. Having a line or two on a Saturday night was as standard as buying the Mirror and reading it with a cup of tea on a Sunday morning for me and Dave. It had become the norm. It had become a way to pass the time. To make us smile. But it had never become any less exciting.

When your heart's racing like a greyhound it's part of the fun to try to race your words against your speeding pulse. But then your thoughts become more dangerous. You're like, ah go on Charlie boy, do your worst.

Each cigarette strengthens your soul. Each line of powder builds your power. Each Tequila sends you catapulting to the edge. But you can handle the edge. You're all over the edge. Ha - what fucking edge?!

Cocaine can turn your sorrow into a sense of pride and indulgence. It can make you both unbreakable and wholly willing to embrace death and darkness.

At least, that's how it feels. I have a terrible feeling on the outside me and Dave look more like 1980s Kylie and Jason on fast-forward with helium.

We eventually left the pub and headed back to mine, screeching Nirvana songs from the top of our tar-ridden lungs at any passer-by who might normally choose not to listen. They had no choice. It was pissing it down, Kurt was dead, and my brain was trying to take on the cruel pathetic world that took him from us – the cruel pathetic world otherwise known as the students, transients and families who were actually trying to get a good night's sleep in the terraced houses that lined my homely little street.

I fumbled around angrily in my canvas bag until I found the keys, dropped them between my muddy boots and eventually got it together enough to open the door. I switched on the light and was instantly welcomed by my beautiful boy Trevor who came charging down the stairs with a pant and a skip. I have to admit, by that point, I had a pang of guilt rising from my gut at being around my little Trev while blatantly under the influence. I therefore needed to rid myself of such parental pain.

'Another line, Emma?'

I opened a cheap bottle of Country Manor wine that had been chilling in the fridge. Not sure why I bothered chilling it, no amount of refrigerated air could hide the vinegary taste and nostril-smarting fumes that exuded from the screw top bottle. Still, it'd do.

Dave kicked off his Adidas and took his usual position on my tired green sofa, while I camped out on the floor, ashtray and wine within easy reach of me and my cheap plastic hi-fi and prized record collection.

Admittedly, I wasn't the best at keeping vinyl in good nick. Dave was always scolding me about how I needed to care for it as though it were made of delicate gold leaf. His vinyl was kept safely in anti-static protective sleeves, and always stored in alphabetical order. He was disciplined with his vinyl. Mine, on the other hand, would amass in a pile of unprotected 12" and 7" discs on the floor, complete with ash and bottle tops, until I cleared it up the following morning.

I took Nirvana's Bleach out of its sleeve and chucked it under the needle.

'Careful' Dave reminded me.

As the heavy basslines of Blew rattled through my tinny speakers (they came with my cheap hi-fi package) even Trev started to look like he was part of the rock scene. The tone in my quaint little living room was moody, and my grief over our beloved rock star palpable. We sat in near silence until the needle finished its work and revolved round and round refusing to pick itself back up off the record.

I let it spin and crackle. Dave had nodded off, peacefully spooning Trev like the romantic couple of the century. This was no Marmite relationship. Meanwhile it hit me – no amount of cocaine, cigarettes or Country Manor wine was going to relieve me of the fact that the night was over.

While my brain was still living the night-time angst with a side of rock 'n' roll, daylight was threatening to infiltrate my soul like an unwelcome visitor that wouldn't stop banging on the door. Time to clean up. Time to exhale the toxins. I looked for some of our traditional 'come-down' tunes in my record collection. The Lightning Seeds. The Breeders. The Cranberries.

I chose the Cranberries. Perhaps Dolores' soothing, otherworldly voice could save me from feeling like shit.

I felt tainted and exposed and ashamed. If I wanted to save myself from darkness and death I'd need to stop chasing them. The music played in the background, but it sounded quiet and insignificant. It no longer gave me the edge I needed. No longer was I consumed and in the moment of rock 'n' roll. There were just tiny fragments of it all around. And separately, in this wholly disconnected way, they couldn't save me from the anxiety that was creeping in.

My heart was pounding and I could feel a slight force and shallowness to my breathing. I looked over at Dave, snoring away peacefully. Was that a rattle I could hear in his breath? We'd smoked far too many cigarettes, and the thought of another made me want to vomit. The thought of booze did, too.

There was no denying it. The night was over.

I needed an antidote. I needed some innocence to make my body good and wholesome again. Why didn't we just sit at mine and watch The Simpsons with a cuppa or something instead of getting wasted down the pub like we do every single weekend. Kurt's passing was a sign to slow down, not speed up.

Perhaps the purity of water might help? A shower, perhaps? But I was too fucked to bother so I just sat there. Record spinning, brain hurting. As my heart fluttered away in chaotic palpitations I started wondering whether I should plan for my imminent demise.

What if tonight was the night? What if I suddenly left this earth, clutching my chest as Dave slept soundly. My poor Trevor would be terrified. But Dave wouldn't wake through his snoring. And this is how I'd be remembered; sitting in a pit of cigarette butts and cheap Country Manor wine and yet I hadn't even released a record, or written poetry or changed a law.

Nope. I might die, right here, in a terraced house in Hull, just some girl who works for a caravan company, typing numbers into boxes.

It made sense that it might happen tonight. My birthday was just a few months away. How could I leave Dad? And Trev? And Dave?

I decided, I either needed to uncover what it was that was putting us all at risk of early death and put a stop to it, or I needed to prepare for the inevitable.

It was too much for my screwy brain to take in at that moment.

Perhaps pizza could save me.

'Hi, yeah, pepperoni please. 10". And chips, yep. Thanks'

CHAPTER 2

Fuck.

I was seriously hungover. Getting up and out of my pit was going to be a challenge.

I felt like a Tory party conference had gate-crashed my brain and all I could do was sit back and listen to the inevitable destruction of my very being and life as we know it. Shit, this is life as we know it. It's 1994 and this is what we, as a country, seemingly pedalling very quickly backwards, chose.

We'd be better off if it was Bob and Brenda presiding over the country. That's what Dad says anyway. I have to agree. They manage to keep The Angel in check anyways and that's no mean feat.

But Brenda did warn me last night. She always knew best. And by that, I mean, she really *does* know best. The day I start listening to her is the day I stop feeling like this. And the day she and Bob lose the bulk of their Tequila takings.

She was very pragmatic when Mum had the affair. They'd been good friends – I remember that because she'd sometimes come to ours and dance around the lounge to the Beatles, fuelled by Babycham, when Dad was keeping Bob company at the pub.

After the revelations about the affair, when Dad was feeling cheated and heartbroken, Brenda would come and sit with me allowing Dad some 'bloke' time with Bob (aka drowning his sorrows). She was never especially cuddly or indulgent. But her no-nonsense words somehow made me feel stronger. She uses them to this day. And she can always get a good read of me. Which can be pretty unnerving at times.

I was beginning to wish I had heeded her warnings last night. My heart was still racing from the clash of toxins I put into my body. And the bathroom bin smelt so badly of Diamond White and pepperoni I was gagging from the stench from the other side of the house.

It didn't help that I'd dropped my work keys into the mix. Fishing those out of a toxic bin full of rotten apple-flavoured vom, used bits of dental floss and too many Tampax applicators (it's hard to direct them comfortably to their target when you've had one too many) wasn't what I needed first thing in the morning.

Seriously, though. Cocaine. Tequilas. What am I, 17?

I woke up with Kurt Cobain's face on my pillow (so much for saving that mint edition of Melody Maker as a souvenir) and one foot in a Luigi's Takeaway pizza box with only half a pepperoni pizza for company. At least my heel enjoyed an overnight tomato-based cleanse.

I had unfortunately discovered, however, that it's pretty tricky getting the tomato tint off hard scaly skin. I was the proud owner of tomato-flavoured lizard feet. Neither Kurt Cobain or Jim Morrison would have been lining up to give me a toe job any time soon.

I made a mental note to grab some emergency Body Shop potions when the nausea subsided. Which, based on its current determination, I was guessing would be at some point in the next week.

So for now, my feet were to remain tinged-red and scaly. Scaly feet, chaotic thoughts and a stomach that thinks it's moshing at a Metallica gig.

This too shall pass. Enter light. Please!

This is exactly the thing I'm talking about. I needed to start living a healthier lifestyle. I needed to be the fresh-faced joggers running through the park at 6am, not the green-faced wreck walking back from Spiders nightclub as is often the case.

I always hated seeing them. I despised them. The joggers

that is. Not because I looked down on them. But because they made me look down upon myself. And when you're already stricken with the fear, that's really not a good thing to be forced to do.

I felt toxic and tainted. I needed to stop all this rubbish. I was 26 – I should've known better. And it's not like I had long to sort my life out before the big 2-7 crept up on me with a sledgehammer or whatever it decided to finish me off with.

I was too old for cocaine. Everyone's too old for cocaine. Jesus Christ what have I been putting in my body all these years?

I vowed never to take cocaine ever again.

Dave reckons his hangovers don't get him like this.

'Yeah I feel battered after a big one,' he said when I once casually dropped into conversation my palpitations, sense of impending doom and feelings of acute poisoning tantamount to an arsenic overdose, 'but it tends to fuck off with a Nurofen and a packet of cheese n onion'.

He's so matter of fact about stuff. It's like, yep, that happens, and then it goes, and that's that.

I wish I could be more Dave.

However, I wasn't. And instead I had a big dark cloud of doom hanging over my hangover.

I trundled down the stairs with Trev in tow to confront whatever wreck I'd left in the front room and stick some light-hearted tunes on, only to be jolted out of my apathetic state by Trevor barking furiously. I tried to adjust my eyes – I'm sure tequila has the potential to blind you.

What the…?

'Dave! What's happened to you?'

I had forgotten that he'd fallen asleep on the sofa. Last night was all a bit of a blur. Last I remember is Dave happily spooning Trev and snoring contentedly. I do not remember anything that would have suggested I might be greeted by the abomination that was currently standing right in front of me. And Trev, blatantly, did not recognise the strange aura radiating from Dave's head. It's like he'd overdosed on Ready Brek, but only in the head department.

'Emma. What have I done?'

'I don't know Dave, what have you done!?'

'I remember waking up to go to the loo, and I saw it in the bathroom. And I thought…why not?'

The once subtle mid-brown curtain hairstyle that flopped casually over Dave's eyes a la Shaun Ryder was now, suddenly, orange.

'You've been at my Sun-in hair spray haven't you? How much have you used?'

'I figured one application would be, like, one bottle, so…'

'Um, yeah, maybe on Rapunzel. Jesus Dave, even I only use a few squirts in the summer. You've got like, 5 inches of hair at most.'

'I was drunk. I don't know. And why does it feel like…like straw.'

As he touched his now bright orange curtains I could practically hear the frazzle as strands disintegrated in between his fingertips. His curtains had been starched to death.

'You're gonna have to get a haircut, Dave. It's curtains for your curtains I'm afraid.'

I let out a chuckle but quickly realised that Dave wasn't as jovial about the whole incident as I was. But it is funny when you think about it. Men often look like they haven't tried to get the look they have. They look effortlessly cool. Because there's no make-up or satin or high heels. But we forget that this effortless look has indeed been the result of careful consideration. It must have taken a while for Dave to perfect his Happy Monday's-esque hair. Just like it will have taken a while for him to wear his Adidas Sambas in. And now, in one fell swoop, his indie charm had been replaced with…

'I look like Worzel Gummidge.'

And with that I couldn't help myself. I collapsed on the sofa in a still-slightly-drunk heap of laughter and Dave headed out the door. I peeked out of the window to watch him hurrying down the street, head down, his usual casual swagger replaced by a half-run. Poor Dave.

Still, it helped distract me from my hungover anguish.

I couldn't be bothered with tidying so the living room was to remain less than minimalist for the day. Friday's dirty plate was still on the wooden coffee table, complete with a rapidly solidifying dollop of ketchup, a few fish-finger crumbs and the bits of chips I'd cut off because they had eyes in them. And my Saturday night post-pub vinyl binge was apparent given the fact they were spread out all over the floor.

I shut the curtains well before dark, turned on the lamp to warm me back up with its glow, dragged my patchwork print duvet downstairs and tapped the edge of the sofa to let Trev know he was welcome too. He soon jumped up and joined me in my hangover self-sympathy session, complete with a Cornish pasty I'd forgotten was in the fridge. Bonus.

What a sorry state I was, curled up in a ball on my sofa, cheap pastry crumbs making their way to my belly button from my pyjama vest top, the 14" TV on mute with page after page of Teletext seemingly stuck on a loop in the background.

There's only one thing worse than daytime telly, and that's Teletext. Even the 'Fun and Games' section had limited ability to entertain me. And Bamboozle was not a game that could be played when you'd killed off a load of brain cells.

I certainly couldn't face listening to the sounds of Seattle and Minneapolis today. If rock music was killing people off, perhaps I really did need to stay away. Perhaps I needed to embrace a more clean-cut night out. Pop is clean-cut, right? A hubba-bubba of smiley happy fun?

I wasn't a teenager anymore. I needed to go out to dinner parties, drink Chardonnay and talk politics. I needed more sophistication and less cocaine. It was time for all this nonsense to stop. I needed to hunt down a rock-free pop palace and find some solace.

Weirdly, the darkness of rock music suddenly felt less endearing. Instead of being a friend who really got what I was going through, it became a dreadful taunt. A stark reminder of my mortality. Of everyone's mortality.

Would rock music be the death of me?

When I pulled myself out of hangover hell, I called Dave and mooted the idea of a change of scenery. Somewhere lighter and brighter to try out on a spring weekend night. Somewhere to meet new people. Somewhere to resurrect the kind of dance routines I learnt as a kid. Somewhere a bit cleaner where the punters don't do so much naughty stuff.

But he was less than enthusiastic when I suggested we attend Hull's most neon nightclub, LA's, next Friday.

Of course, I didn't tell him that this was all driven by my fear of joining the 27-club. That I wanted to try out a different, more light-hearted, safer lifestyle, to see if it suited me. He had no time whatsoever for superstition. You couldn't get more straight-up than Dave. And he wasn't about to let a ladder interrupt his stride.

LA's was, and always had been, off limits. So this would require some serious persuasion tactics.

'We're in our mid-twenties and we've avoided it our entire lives, Emma.'

But like I said, I needed to change my diet. I needed to re-divert my destiny to a place of safety. Pop stars didn't die aged 27. I mean, look at Cliff Richard, he's still going. I needed to see what the world of pop was like. To see if I could stomach it. But no way was I entering into that foreign and synthetic world all alone.

It hurt my eyes just thinking about it. All those neon

lights. And I wasn't exactly relishing the idea of dancing around a handbag either. Besides, I wasn't sure they'd let me get away with stomping around a canvas rucksack in my boots.

I was used to sitting in dark, smoky bars with a live band spraying beer all over the front row. And that's precisely how people get electrocuted by their electric guitar. I can't see the Pet Shop Boys or Erasure getting electrocuted. They look like they respect their organs. Keyboards, I mean.

Apologies for the outdated pop music references, by the way. I'm one of those dick-head people who refuses to acknowledge that they know what's in the charts.

OK. Take That. D:ream. Shaggy. I've heard them all. I know all the words. It's not exactly my fault they're there every morning blasting out on the radio breakfast show when the alarm goes off. They worm their way into your brain before you've regained full consciousness.

Experiencing the pop music clubs, however, is something else entirely. And neon is quite possibly the best descriptor. For the venue, the make-up and the men's shirts.

No wonder they wore sunglasses inside.

Dave was coming with me whether he liked it or not. You can't travel alone to a whole new stomping ground.

I told him I was just desperately bored. That I needed a change of scenery. That we'd done all the dive pubs to death and we needed a new experience. We needed to meet new people. And we would not be going to Spiders after The Angel this week. We'd be trialling LA's.

'Seriously, Emma. Are you feeling alright? This is totally out of character. And out of the blue, might I add.'

He took a lot of persuading, but eventually, he agreed. I always had a back-up plan. I knew what his kryptonite was. I knew he couldn't resist the sound of the Gallagher brothers. So I bribed him with tickets for an Oasis gig.

In Hull would you believe?

I couldn't quite believe it when I heard the news that they were coming to The Adelphi – our little live music bar in a residential terraced street in Hull.

That place was immense. The bar was basically the front of a bus and you'd be served through the missing bus window. And the air was so smoky and loud you felt like you must have some serious punk rock credentials if you could walk into the place and emerge with more than 50% of your hearing still intact.

The Adelphi was basically an end terrace. I always wondered who lived next door? Or had they kept it empty for post-gig groupie gatherings and a cheap place for the bands to crash? Whoever was running it made sure it would earn legendary status though. It might not be glamorous, but the names that went through that door were something else.

Could I really cut myself off from my beloved Adelphi? Could I really miss Oasis at our gorgeously tatty little music club in favour of Re-wind High School dance classics with a free alco-pop thrown in?

I would miss our tiny little music club if I severed all ties. But I needed to change my diet and clean out my lungs - and my mind - from all the dark stuff. The death of Kurt Cobain triggered a feeling in me I couldn't quite describe or indeed shake off. A feeling of dread. Of dreadful inevitability. As though I was destined to lose myself in the relentless darkness. An unnerving feeling of Deja vu.

I needed this antidote; I needed some straightforward, surface area pop music. How could I break it to Dave that he might be going to see the Gallagher brothers alone?

But that didn't matter right now. All that mattered was that he said yes to LA's.

'OK, Emma.'

Even if he managed to sigh loudly while speaking those three tiny syllables.

But if Oasis were involved…

He once agreed to buy the drinks all night if I stepped away from the juke box and let him put Oasis on a loop. So, to see them live in his hometown and have his mate buy the tickets….it was a no brainer. It was what he had been waiting for his entire life. That was Dave's inevitable destiny. That's what kept Dave going.

When the big Friday night came around – the night we were to pop our LA's cherry – I decided I needed a little Dutch courage and a makeover to get me in the mood.

I legged it to town after work and headed straight to Hull's answer to Rodeo Drive – a little street lined with boutique clothes shops. I knew of a little independent shop down there that Claire from work always raved about – a place that sold clubwear in every manner of style. From floor length satin halter neck dresses, to two-piece skirts and crop top combos in shiny elasticated fabrics.

I went inside and, although I was admittedly taken aback by the prices, I decided it might be worth splashing out a little to get the right outfit. There didn't seem to be anyone else in there – not even a sales assistant, but I figured they must be out the back or something.

I was just holding up a chiffon and Lycra black and sheer floor length dress, when a voice came from nowhere behind me.

'The shop is closed. Please leave.'

I turned around. It was the owner of the shop. I knew it was him because he was usually stood by the front door.

'Oh.' I said. 'But the door was open?'

'The shop is closed. Leave now.'

He practically ushered me out the door and slammed it shut behind me. He still didn't put the 'closed' sign on, but he just stood there, glaring at me. It was like a scene from Pretty Woman, but with a little more aggression.

I shrugged and walked off down the street. A lady was just closing her shop up a couple of doors down and she'd obviously seen the confused look on my face.

'He just chuck you out, love?'

'Yeah. What's that about?'

'He obviously doesn't like the look of you. He's done it to a few people. You should be thankful, though. My daughter once went in and he locked her in! Hung around the dressing room whilst she was trying things on. Sometimes it's good not to be attractive to certain men.'

I wasn't quite sure how to take that. I looked down at what I was wearing. I'd headed to town straight from work so, yes, I wasn't at my most glamorous. I was wearing a shirt, a little A-line skirt and Dr Martens shoes, complete with a denim jacket and my canvas bag. But I thought I looked alright. Still, at least I was kicked out, not locked in. What a weirdo! Perhaps there were risks to this new found world I was about to enter. Maybe the risks weren't solely aligned to rock music. I had to find out either way, though.

I didn't have long left until all the bigger chains shut so I headed towards the bus station and darted into C&A just over the road. I had a vague idea that something made of satin would help me blend right in – and it wasn't long before I found a bright red satin floaty mini skirt on the sales rail. It immediately made me think of Supergirl, which I thought could only be a good thing.

I sourced a black velvet choker to accessorize and a green sparkly cropped top to finish off my look. My work at C&A done, I headed back home on the bus, jumping off a stop early to grab a bottle of Diamond White cider from the offie. At 7.5% it was the perfect post-tea beverage to calm the nerves. And it was as close to alcopop as I was prepared to get.

I walked and fed Trev, wolfed down a Lean Cuisine then drained the Diamond White whilst listening to a compilation consisting of Technotronic, Black Box and 2 Unlimited (an 'ironic' gift from Dave one Christmas).

As Technotronic 'pumped up the jam', I pumped up my lips with a liner two shades darker than my lipstick, and attempted to formulate some respectable townie dance moves in my full length mirror (I knew all about the 'big fish, little fish, cardboard box' move – it was win-win – a dance move with easy to follow instructions).

It wasn't until I was leaving the house that I realised I hadn't invested in suitable shoes and jacket – so, inspired by cider-induced confidence, I shrugged it off, pulled on my docs and grabbed my black velvet jacket.

I met Dave in The Angel to give us time to drown out whatever cynicism was still lurking in our guts. He'd 'dealt' with his glowing straw-like mop and wasn't looking especially happy about it. I'm not sure he even went to the barbers for that. I think he'd maybe just taken his shavers to it. In the light, you could still see a flame-coloured tinge on the edges of his now almost shaven head. He really did have that ReadyBrek glow now.

By the time I got there, Dave had already knocked back a few pints of beer as Dutch courage, propping up the bar and telling Brenda and Doreen all about my 'crazy idea'. I could instantly see that he wasn't exactly chomping at the bit for a piece of LA's.

They all watched me as I walked in. I was attempting to look as I did any other night even though I'd switched my usual band t-shirt for the bright green crop top that left my midriff feeling vulnerable (and me feeling paranoid that my belly button had transported cake crumbs from my on-the-go Skelton's pudding).

Brenda looked at me curiously as I approached the bar.

'So what's this all about then Emma? Why you dragging poor Dave to town? And what did you do to his hair?'

Lying bastard! Still, given the look he threw me, a kind of panicked puppy dog plea, I decided to let it go. He was doing me a favour tonight after all.

'It was with the best of intentions, Bren.'

We never ventured into town. LA's was surrounded by pre-club pubs that played Abba mixed with hardcore rave.

'You two kids be careful.' She said. Brenda always thought we were softer than the other punters. A point on which Dave often felt he needed to prove her wrong on after a few beers.

'Yer dunno what'cherr t-talking about Bren. Bring me a f-fightery and we'll see who's sorry. I'll sher yer Bren. Jush you watch love.'

You knew Dave was pissed if he called Brenda 'love'. It was only a few steps from 'love' to falling asleep under the 'sitteries'.

But he wasn't giving it large tonight. If anything, his beer was making him seem more serious as he drank it. Then Doreen raised her glass of stout. 'Here's to life' before resuming her position of simply sitting in silence and grinning like a Cheshire cat.

I've no idea what she meant. She appeared to have had a good few milk stouts by this point. It might not have even been in reference to our brave townie voyage at all. She might not have even been listening. She could often disappear into her own world. And it always looked like a nice little world judging by the smile on her face.

Doreen had lived a life. Sure, she was getting on a bit, but she always had an air of experience and authority about her. She'd sit with her milk stouts and her slimline Davidoff cigarettes that she had shipped to order from Crete or wherever, and her commentary on the pub conversation was always succinctly powerful.

I always imagined it would be great to see Doreen go up against Thatcher in a debate. She'd kill her dead with one-word responses and a smile on her face.

She'd mix her 1940s wartime clothing with random elements of today's fashion. So you'd often see her in a belted dress, trench coat, a pair of Fila trainers and a crushed velvet hat. She played by nobody's rules. And given her rather unhealthy lifestyle (she was in the pub literally every single day) I could only deduce that her mind and her body were the literal depiction of hardcore. Nothing would break our Doreen.

She was open to whatever took her fancy. Whatever the trends of the decades threw at her, she'd try. She was in her early fifties when Hendrix died, but she still saw him live before it happened and she bloody loved it. I was over the moon when I introduced her to Babes in Toyland and she said the lead singer was a brilliant role model. Quite a different reaction to that of my dad's whenever he heard me playing their angry sounds. Doreen said anyone who screams that a rapist is 'dead meat motherfucker' was OK in her book.

Doreen always said that there was no point living life like a 'good little girl' when you could be enjoying yourself. And she's showing no signs of giving up any time soon. So why was it a different story for so many others? Why didn't *they* make it into their 70s?

I might not have been especially looking forward to a night of pop, but I thought it was a safer alternative and therefore possibly worth the sacrifice. At least I did until Brenda's eyes darted to my feet as she walked by collecting glasses: 'your choice of footwear might not go down very well, love.'

I looked down at my feet but tried to remain confident and resolute.

'What do you mean? I always wear these boots.'

'Exactly' she said. 'But not to LA's. Nobody wears Dr Martens in LA's.'

'I'll be fine'. I said. Surely a pair of boots can't be the definitive marker of who a person really is?

Brenda had spent many a night in LAs before taking on The Angel. Her stomping ground was always the centre of town. The home of foam parties, halter-neck tops and too much Taboo and lemonade, which was ironic really because not many things were taboo in town. Brenda knew exactly what to expect and exactly how to dance to the likes of Erasure (sorry, Take That). Whereas our stomping ground was usually dodgy clubs like Spiders in the middle of derelict industrial estates that let in underaged middle class kids with conflict across their faces and tie dye across their t-shirts.

And then there was us. It's hard to fit in when you live in a small terrace in Hull and don't comply with the in-crowd's music regulations. But Dave and I had both grown up with Dad's musical influences so we were kind of stuck. Bomb the Bass and D Mob just didn't do it for us. The cry of 'Acieed' just gave me a headache.

Still, if there was one place not to fit in, it was Spiders nightclub and we'd been going since we were kids. The uninspiring flat-roofed building nestled into a Hull industrial estate that accommodated the punks, goths and, let's be honest, teeny-boppers who enjoyed a bit of Neds Atomic Dustbin and Bjork. People desperately tried not to fit in in there, so we were onto a winner before we even arrived.

The anticipation of our new night out reminded me of the time Dave and I were going into town for the first time without adult supervision. We were ten. And Dave had the tenner my dad had given him for his birthday.

As we left the house, Dad scruffed Dave's hair, stuck an extra quid in my pocket and smartened my anorak by pulling it up over my shoulders. 'Be careful you two.'

And of course, we were fine. We got on and off the bus no problem. And we spent all of Dave's money in precisely 47 seconds on Panini football stickers in the nearest newsagents. We then sat in a café drinking a cup of tea (very grown up – except for the amount of sugar that we poured in) whilst seeing if we could finally fill his sticker album.

We had, of course, wanted lemonade, but decided we needed to embrace our newfound grown-up-ness. It's like when you really want to dance to Kylie, but you're in company, so your only option is to shoegaze in a melancholy manner to The Jesus and Mary Chain.

Why is happiness so uncool?

Sadly, even though we had bought a tenner's worth of stickers that day, we were still missing Brian Clough and West Bromwich Albion. And we couldn't afford another cup of tea, or indeed a lemonade, to sweeten our day.

We trundled back home feeling deflated and, after that, Panini sticker books went right down in our estimation. I don't think we ever bought another packet. Not even when Smash Hits brought them out. Of course, Dave kept that book, but there are still two gaps to this day. It always reminds us of our first failed trip to town. It was about the content, not the getting there and back, after all.

I had a feeling that LA's might be the same. Getting there obviously wouldn't be the issue. Enjoying it, on the other hand, felt like quite a stretch. And I had no idea how to dance to Shaggy.

We left The Angel and got the bus to town. We hopped off at the lights, crossed the road and walked towards LA's. Strangely, I didn't have that familiar feeling of excitement that anything could happen. It was more a strange feeling of doom that anything could happen. And the 'anything' wasn't going to include having fun. But I was determined to at least see how the other half lived.

The queue was huge - I had no idea this place was so in demand. We moved gingerly to the back of the keyed-up queue, attracting many a suspicious look as we walked past the eager regulars.

We kept our heads down and barely spoke.

'What the fuck were you thinking.' Dave muttered, keeping his head facing forward at all times.

'It's different, though. A change. And look at all the people here. They obviously love it. How can a billion Hull people be wrong? So we might love it when we get in there.' I'm not sure who I was trying to convince.

He didn't even reply. We stood at the back of the queue. Silently. We could hear the music from inside the club pulsating with poppy beats. D:ream came on.

'Fuck's sake, Emma.'

He lit up a ciggie. His hand was shaking. Who knew Dave could get nervous about a night out? I was OK, after all, if I wanted to make it to the next general election, I needed a change of scenery. And this was the antithesis of punk rock. These fuckers would live forever.

'They're all staring at your boots, Emma.'

He was shifting uncomfortably. We saw more of this strange, foreign tribe joining the queue. Shirts were indeed brightly coloured. There was leopard print, but not in a punk rock way because it was teamed with handbags with gold chain straps. The air was thick with Lynx aftershave. Crop tops, Lycra and stiletto heels walked past us excitedly. Confidently. I'd forgotten what confidence was.

'This is a highly responsible social experiment, Dave' I whispered. 'It's like the Northern Ireland peace process talks.' I added, tenuously. Instantly regretting comparing something like that to attempting to participate in the world of pop music in a neon-lit building.

But there were indeed always tribal conflicts in high school relating to your musical taste. We were called 'grebs' because we wore Dr Martens. They were called 'townies' because they wore shiny shoes and bright colours. But surely, we were all just people. And surely, now, we were all grown up.

'Grebs!'

The call came from a group of lads walking by. Dave lit another ciggie with the one he'd almost burnt to the filter. In about three drags.

'Fuck's sake, Emma.'

There was laughter from the crowd. And comments about me not washing. God, it really was like high school all over again. Is this what alcopops do to grown-ups?

I was about to open my mouth and shout something back but Dave noticed my imminent stupidity and stamped on my toes, giving me a stern look. Even my Dr Martens failed to protect me from the force of Dave's Adidas.

The queue was gradually moving forward and the music was getting louder. And tinnier. Snogging was already in full flow under the cloud of LuLu perfume and Lynx aftershave.

I was a Bodyshop Dewberry girl. And, according to a passer-by, I smelt of hippies.

'Fucking hell, Emma'. A shake of the head accompanied the mutter this time.

The bouncer waved the group in front of us through the bright, seemingly pulsating silver doors. Then he put a big, stern hand up in front of Dave.

What on earth had he done to warrant that?

'No trainers mate.'

'No worries' said Dave, seeming rather more chipper all of a sudden and turning with a spring in his step. And that was that. We left the club. And headed to Spiders. An altogether different vibe.

As I rummaged in my back pocket for my red cardboard Spiders membership card, I noticed Dave had already disappeared through the doors. I showed my card, paid my entry fee and found him at the bar, ordering two pangalactic gargleblasters.

'I don't care what you say, Emma. We deserve this. And we deserve Metallica.'

As I took a seat in a caged spider's web and lit up a cigarette, I told myself, this was the last time I was going to dance with the Devil.

After the dismal attempt at pop music, I started to wonder if maybe music genre wasn't the problem. Maybe that was like changing from whiskey to lager. It wasn't sorting out the core issue, it was just chasing after another problem. A different problem. Maybe it doesn't matter what nightclub I'm in. The truth is, I should just stay home. Stay out of trouble. Stop throwing up pangalactic gargleblasters of a morning.

It was time to embrace the telly. After The Angel, of course.

I'm not a kid anymore. And perhaps therein lies the very problem. There's another theory, you see. It's all about the Saturn return.

Apparently, in astrology, the planet Saturn has a 29-year orbit. And it returns to the original sign in our birth chart between the ages of 28 and 30. So its influence is felt from about the age of...you guessed it - 27.

This book I picked up said that, psychologically, the first Saturn return is the moment we reach full adulthood. And of course, that's a pretty tricky thing to deal with. And perhaps that's why so many rock stars struggle with it. Because adults are just not equipped with the stamina to play out all night like they used to.

When you're a kid you feel invincible. You won't get cancer from smoking Lambert and Butler. You won't drop dead by taking an E. You won't get the clap by sleeping with Brett Donovan from sixth form.

And then, all of a sudden, while you're doing the same things you've always done, enjoying yourself and having a laugh, your eyes open. And you realise the risks involved in having fun. It's not all theoretical. And on top of managing all that, you're rapidly approaching thirty and you really shouldn't be asking your dad to lend you the money for this month's phone bill.

The bell was ringing for the end of playtime. It was time to grow up. But I was starting to wish I hadn't lost my innocence quite so young. What if the damage was already done?

Ugh. I needed a drink.

CHAPTER 3

Why that song. Every. Single. Morning. Don't Viking chuffing Radio have anything else to play at 08:08?

Yep, we have a grey-faced Tory Prime Minister, Kevin Costner is apparently the closest thing we've got to Robin Hood, our poet is dead (RIP Kurt) and it's Monday bastard morning so, you're right, D:Ream, things *can* only get better. But do you have to tell me *every single morning.*

If your alarm clock makes you so angry that you slam the off button with intense fury, falling instantly back to sleep, missing your breakfast, forgetting to walk Trevor and having the mother of all headaches, it's really not fit for purpose.

I'm setting it for 08:13 tomorrow in the hope I can bypass D:Ream and wake up to something else.

Today did not get off to a good start. And it certainly *didn't* get better.

I didn't spend three years at university to sit in a grey office with a plastic plant, typing up sales invoices for caravans bought by people who are, for some inexplicable reason, desperate to purchase a spare room on a cramped campsite in Withernsea. I don't get it. Buy a camper van and you can go anywhere you like. Why the fuck choose static? Houses are static. It's like having a mini house. Stuck in a flat grass field by the dreary North Sea.

But still, the money pours into these static little plots less than 20 miles down the road where you're highly likely to spend your leisure time with Kev 'n' Linda from number 57 – the very people you're trying to escape from – in a too-close-for-comfort indoor jacuzzi experience with a bottle of Lambrini cos it's lashing down outside. Again.

I just couldn't get passionate about static caravans. On-site jacuzzi or no on-site jacuzzi. Sorry, but working somewhere and not enjoying it gives you a negative view of the industry. To me, caravans meant Monday morning.

Problem is, it's not just the industry that bores me.

I'd be bored if I was typing up invoices for the Serious Organised Crime Agency, never mind Shaw's Static Holiday Homes.

I needed a challenge. Something to excite me. Something to test me.

However, my destiny seemed to be spending five days a week eating Jaffa Cakes with Claire, typing numbers into boxes in front of the words 'berth', 'manufacturer's warranty' and 'excluding VAT' and downing can after can of Diet Coke to get me from 9am to 5pm without having to stick pins through my eye lids.

It's hardly what you might call a purposeful job.

Christ, even if we were giving caravans away to the homeless, my role in the business would still be insignificant. Gordon the Gopher could type numbers into boxes. A brain workout it is not.

When I was at university I loved writing. And I loved English classes at school. I always had a thing for using words to find the answer to a problem. To dissect information and investigate conclusions. Testing and probing information then translating it all into something interesting to read.

Numbers into boxes doesn't really cut it.

Claire's a sweetheart though. It's Claire, along with the cans of Diet Coke, that always help me get through the sales admin monotony. She always had a tale to tell and under that brash exterior she flaunts she definitely has a heart of gold.

She joined the company just before I did, so we've always had each other's backs. We look like a mis-matched couple – Claire with her permed hair and scrunchies, whilst my dark hair fell lank down the back of my shoulders. Claire would arrive in smart high heels, pencil skirt and low-cut blouse, whilst I wore my Dr Marten's shoes, thick woollen tights and corduroy A-line miniskirt. On the outside we were complete opposites, but we shared quite a few opinions on life. Especially on life at Shaw's Static Holiday Homes.

I worry about Claire, though. Her life seems to be a revolving merry-go-round of flashing her boobs in LAs on a Saturday night after downing too many Blue WKDs then heaving them all back up on the shiny shoes of one of Humberside's finest police officers, before ordering chips and gravy from the catering van outside and heading home with a virtual stranger.

It's funny that the more grown-up the appearance, the more childlike the response to drink.

Meh, who was I to talk?

If you changed the venue from LAs to Spiders and the music from D:Ream to Sonic Youth, we weren't that different. It just so happened that I was puking up on someone's Beetle Crusher's at the end of the night instead. I couldn't handle my drink, I just needed the oblivion sometimes. I'm guessing it was the same for Claire. I should have really thought about that before assuming that LAs was a safe space away from debauchery and excess. It's really not. So why the hell do pop stars appear to live for longer?

Every Monday morning it was the same. Tales from town. The re-telling of Claire's adventures took us from 08:30 right through to lunch time, and she only stopped briefly for a sausage roll and a can of Tango before we'd be back in the 'he said', 'she said' pre-shag scene setting.

It was either Dan from Friday night or Paul from Saturday night and she was constantly changing her mind about which one she wanted to call her that week.

I guess neither Dan nor Paul wore trainers to nightclubs.

Turn off. Tune out. Cop off.

The more I got to know Claire, the more I realised that the bravado and comedic, outrageous tale-telling was a front to show she was in total control. And she was in control of her antics, but perhaps she wasn't in control of what was *driving* her antics.

I'm not sure Claire was all that happy, really.

I was incredibly grouchy. My hangover (from the impromptu Sunday teatime trip to the pub) decided to hang-over for 48 hours (possibly because the weekend's hair of the dog was, in all honesty, more the entire dog than the hair) and I was feeling rancid.

But the sales team's conversation is far, far more nauseating than a hangover could ever be. I'd love to stick the entire sales office in Room 101.

Told you I loved English classes. I never forgot George Orwell.

It's ironic really. Sales is about building effective relationships with prospective customers. So why employ complete wankers like Shane in the role of Sales Manager?

It's a never-ending cycle of cringe.

You get wankers doing sales who blag their way up the ranks and employ more wankers to do more sales, until you end up with one big massive wank stain of a sales department.

And let's be clear what I mean by the term 'wanker'.

Wankers embrace the role of wanker with immense passion. However, wankers do not know they are wankers. They *think* they are VIPs.

They wear far too much Fahrenheit aftershave that, ironically, causes the body temperature of most women to dip below zero.

Shame it didn't cause my mum's temperature to dip below zero. The smell of the sales office always takes me back to the row Mum and Dad had one night. She'd come home in her favourite sparkly jumper, a little tipsy, grabbing me and my Dad for a big bear hug before Dad pushed her away, inquiring about the smell on her top.

It wasn't her usual smell, he said. She smelt like a wanker, he said.

And why are wankers always more successful in the workplace? My dad was a superstar, a hard grafter, but he always missed out on the promotions. Sadly, he didn't miss out on being a part of the 'dead wood cull' as he called it.

I felt as though the wankers in my office were the same as the wanker my mum was 'courting'. All show and no substance.

Shane wore a terrible plastic-looking leather jacket and terrible ties. The tie, I believe, is to prove that he can wear what he wants and do what he likes, because it usually had some ridiculous cartoon-like pattern on it.

And, to top off wanker-dom Shane and co wink at you, hold out their empty coffee mugs with a shake and call you 'love'.

Fuck. Off. And get your own cup of coffee.

But where are the saleswomen?

I'll tell you where they are. They've gone. Because nobody in wanker-dom will promote them. For all that bravado, it's hilarious to think how scared they are of us women in reality.

We know too much. About life, about human nature, about society, about *them*.

Shane leant on Claire's desk drinking a coffee (which neither of us made I hasten to add) with sycophantic sales executive, Bri (who *did* make the coffee), who was behaving like an over-excited puppy, desperate to hear all about Shane's eventful night in LAs.

Thank God they didn't let me and Dave in.

Unluckily for Shane, however, they *did* let Claire in. She was right there. And she saw him in his luminous yellow shirt and Argos-gold necklace getting short shrift from Debs from accounts. So bragging about fingering her in the middle of the dancefloor to Shabba Ranks' '*Mr*

Loverman' while his wife was in the loos is a slight exaggeration of the truth.

Poor cow. I think if my man was planning to cheat on me I'd have more respect for him if he actually managed to go through with it. Begging a colleague on the dancefloor to let you finger them and getting a slap in response is nowt to shout about.

When I think about it, that whole world of fluorescent shirts, cheap aftershave and alcopops is possibly more dark and edgy than Spiders and The Adelphi if you dig a little deeper. On reflection, while the lights might be brighter, so is the sexism. In fact, l can't work out why Claire spends all her Friday nights in that neon-lit cheese-dive.

But she'd say the same to me about Spiders, I guess. Horses for courses. Spiders for webs. Whatever. It's not like I'm going back to either any time soon anyway – for two very different reasons.

I was now needing a major detox from the sleaze-fest discussion at work as well as the booze-fest shenanigans of the weekend. Although to be frank, the chitter chatter was driving me towards a desire for yet more weekend shenanigans. But as that was a while off, I could have that argument with myself on Friday. In the meantime, more of this.

Remember when you were a kid, and Newsround came on and all you could think about was Top of the Pops? Weekdays are my Newsround.

And it was four whole days 'til Friday. Kill me in the face.

I needed a beer after work. Just the one. So we dragged me dad to the pub. School night or no school night, me and Trev caught him eating another Vesta Ready Meal while watching Brookside on his lonesome again when I called in. Leaving him in those circumstances would have been tantamount to abuse. Crispy noodles or no crispy noodles.

I called Dave from Dad's and he said he'd meet us in ten. Dad had no choice now, he was getting his arse off that bloody chair like it or not.

We wandered along to the Angel with Trev in tow and, as we walked through the door, Bob and Brenda looked over the moon to see Dad.

'How's tricks Tel?'

'Ah you know. Pint please, Bren.'

Dad wasn't exactly gushing. He wasn't even talking in full sentences. I ordered a packet of KP nuts to lift his mood when Brenda, having just formed the perfect head on a pint of lager and plonked it on the bar in front of Dad, quickly turned her attention to the man and woman walking through the door.

'Better not be seafood again, Trace. The punters get pissed and leave it to rot on my bloody Axminster.'

'Don't worry, Bren. We're just flogging denim today. Got some great pairs from Kingston Jeanery.'

'Ooh lovely. I'll get my Bob to take a look. Bob. Bob!'

It was Tracey and Pete. Sister and brother who still lived together despite being in their 50s. They spent most of their spare time hawking goods in pubs – whether it be mussels and winkles, or jeans and socks. They had limited success in each bar, but always made enough to buy themselves a pint each before heading off to the next. Tracey always did the talking. Pete barely said a word. They were a funny pair.

Dave arrived and, as per usual, we all took a polite look through the jeans on offer before making our excuses about having no dosh on us. To be fair, Tracey put in a valiant effort when she tried to flog my dad a pair of baggy jeans with a multi-coloured motif of a cartoon kangaroo smoking a spliff on the back pocket (*'they're very you, Tel'*), and her denim bum-bag pitch to me and Dave was admirable (*'you can throw your ciggies, your money and your house keys in them when you got to that arachnid club you're always on about'*)

If there's one thing that might lead to us having our Spiders membership cards removed it was wearing matching denim bum-bags.

After they left, we managed to sup our drinks and order another round, and Dad visibly cheered up thanks to Dave's match analysis banter, so Dad was kept entertained and the ladies were spared Dave's clumsy one-liners.

Things took an uncomfortable turn, however, when we played Dave's 'five things you'd do to get on TV' game in tribute to 'The Hopefuls' slot on late night show The Word - which was both abhorrent and wonderful all at once.

Basically, to beat off stiff competition, contestants had to do the most outrageous thing they could think of to secure their fifteen minutes of fame on the telly. Some of them drank their own vomit, squirted milk from their eyes or snogged a granny.

For our game, we were given five disgusting acts and we'd have to choose one of the five to do on TV. Of course, we weren't going to be going on TV, but it was a way to pass the time.

Dave picked mine:

1. Drink an entire bottle of ketchup in less than five minutes
2. Snog the two old blokes from the Angel
3. Drink Dave's vomit
4. Walk barefoot in Trevor poo
5. Eat a live spider

'Dave, that's rank. Anyway, as if anyone's going to eat a live creature on television. It's animal cruelty. Surely you'd be arrested by the RSPCA or something.'

'So, don't pick that one then!'

'Ugh. It's going to have to be the ketchup then.'

Dad wasn't overly impressed. He still couldn't understand, he said, why we 'kids' liked watching the 'abomination' that is *The Word* on an evening. But me and Dave spent many a late night in front of the box shouting abuse and condemnation at the hopefuls.

'Come on, Tel'. Dave said. 'If we didn't have that to go home to we'd all be gate-crashing your old-man pub lock-ins.'

Dad made a resigned face.

We were so relaxed in each other's company, us three. Dave was as much a part of our family as he is The Angel's.

In fact, you could transport this conversation back two decades and little would have changed, other than the venue. I can see it now, me and Dave, playing in the sand on a beach in Wales. Mum and Dad with their heads back on their deckchairs, supported by a pile of scrunched up, damp, sandy clothes being used as make-shift pillows, huge sunglasses on their faces and tanning oil factor two on their contrasting skin (Mum's skin was always adorably dark, but Dad was pasty white. Well, at the start of the holiday anyway. He usually looked like a prawn cocktail crisp by the end of it). Meanwhile, me and Dave would be sitting by the wind break discussing which superheroes would be allowed in the gang we were about to form to prevent the end of the world as we know it.

There was usually a fair degree of negotiation. I was never a fan of Batman. I didn't like the grey tights. And I always pushed for Wonder Woman to be the leader of the clan.

I loved those holidays with Dave. Mum and Dad invited him every year from when we were tots. I guess with me being an only child, and Dave's much older sister leaving home at 16, it was good for us to have each other. And it meant Mum and Dad had a bit more time to themselves, without having to entertain me non-stop.

We did everything together. And here we were again, heading together down the flaming Drambuie path of no respectable return.

I tried to fool Dad into cutting back on the booze by setting fire to a Pepsi in a shot glass but even he was still sharp enough to realise that there must be a pretty good reason why his was the only shot that wouldn't ignite. And the only one that smelt of cola instead of mince pies.

It does smell of mince pies doesn't it, Drambuie?

I necked mine. I needed it. Never works out well when Dad hits the Drambuie. His political anger becomes all encompassing. Either that, or he'll flirt a little too much with Doreen. Who was blatantly about 30 years his senior and would still eat him for breakfast.

Dad, really.

Of course, it wasn't long before Dad and Bob were giving their usual lecture on socialism to me, Dave and the rest of the pub given the volume of their voices. After that much booze, I was convinced they'd put the voting virgins off altogether.

On Dad's point about Thatcher, one of the two older dudes in raincoats lifted his head from his broadsheet paper and gave my dad a knowing nod, as if to agree, before returning his eyes slowly to the news pages. The body language of those two was the only way we could read them given they never spoke. Well, that and the newspapers they read.

Whenever Dad and Bob were together and there's booze involved this happened. They're like a pair of old tossers in the pub talking bollocks while puffing away on at least three boxes of illegally imported 'Davidoff' ciggies that Bob's mate Ken ships in to order. Doreen always gets hers for free, being the queen of the Angel as she is.

Bob reckons if you can't read the warning signs on the back of an imported cigarette packet then you're entirely immune to any harmful effects. Reckons he'll stop smoking if they put pictures on instead of foreign words. So I guess he's going to be puffing away on Davidoff's tar and arsenic sticks for life then.

Who am I to talk? I can practically feel the tar bubbling up in mine on a night out, then setting like molten rock the day after. My airways are becoming plugged up with a cocktail of Lucky Strike and John Player Special.

I should switch to Silk Cut. It'd be like having a Milky Way instead of a Twix. Milky Way's don't spoil your appetite so surely…Silk Cut don't fuck your lungs up?

I decided that it was either Silk Cut or nothing given I was in my 26th year, in fear of joining the 27 Club, and I'd been smoking for precisely eleven years. That's not a good start for the healthy lifestyle that would protect me from certain death. But you know, baby steps. Who wants to go cold turkey?

By the end of the night I was feeling tired and ready for bed. And this time, there were no Luigi's pizza boxes in sight.

I felt nice and warm and happy, pyjama-clad and cuddling up to Trev in bed.

My beautiful boy. I've no idea what would happen if I ended up meeting someone. I'd feel terrible kicking Trev out of his bedroom. He slept in there with me every night. We were pretty much inseparable. He even sat outside the bathroom when I was on the loo. Dad says Trev's got attachment issues.

I glanced up at my Athena 'L'enfant' print clock – the arms ticking slowly to midnight over the top of one of the most beautiful men in the world (deserving that status thanks to the fact he held a cute little babba – which is always going to make a woman swoon.)

I was sitting up with two chunky pillows behind my back, Trev snuggling in on top of the duvet, reading all about the demise of the tragic Jim Morrison.

The Doors had been recording an album, and Jim Morrison decided to head off to France with Pam, his other half, for some much-needed R&R. But it kind of back-fired because he never returned to the US.

I have mixed feelings about Jim Morrison. Rumour has it that at one point he had 20 paternity suits pending. Twenty!? That's almost one for each year of his short life. And I don't believe any of them related to his girlfriend.

But it's easy, I guess, to imagine that Pam was some kind of long-suffering wife. Maybe, like my mum, she was having all the fun too.

Whatever the case was, it wasn't an especially clean-living lifestyle even if Morrison's last moments were spent in the bath. I wonder if he was trying to cleanse himself of rock 'n' roll? Other than the bath fact however it's all a bit of a mystery. I guess that's because all accounts are so different.

I still couldn't put my finger on what it was about the number 27. There's obviously something they all have in common, but it can't *just* be the number. They all must have something *else* in common, otherwise there would be no such thing as a 28-year-old. And Dad's testament to the fact that they do exist and can in fact progress to a ripe old age.

Over the next few weeks, to make matters worse, I read in NME that another talented star had dropped. Kristen Pfaff. Bassist of Courtney Love's band, Hole. Aged 27. Another band I loved. This couldn't be a coincidence.

You know they say like attracts like? Like, me and Dave, same age, both like the same sort of music. Both have a little darkness to deal with. Both enjoy a few too many bevvies.

Both felt a little isolated from the rest of class, even though we were both pretty well accepted.

It's the same in rock music. Maybe it's about something drawing us all together. Maybe it's about sadness?

With Pfaff, it was another heroin overdose. Another bath tub. Another pained musician. Kristen Pfaff lived for less than a month after turning 27. She was so talented and so pretty. And yet so doomed.

The library books kept drawing me back in and I spent many an evening in my PJs, feet up on the sofa, trying to get my head around whether Kurt Cobain was always destined to kill himself. Could there have been an intervention? Is it what we encounter in life, or is it how we're made that decides our destiny?

What could *I* do to stop it happening to me?

Dave thinks I'm seriously losing it. He thinks I've become obsessed. Says it's all I talk about, and anyway, what's the point of having a cigarette and a beer if I'm not going to enjoy them. If I'm going to spend each drag pondering how many minutes it was going to take from me.

Fair point, I guess. But if I have enough of them, I tend to feel better about things, so…

I actually lied to Dave the other night and told him I'd taken all the music biography books back to the library. Checked them back in early doors. That seemed to placate him. He reckons I've a tendency to get overwhelmed by strange thoughts sometimes. I think he's in denial. Facts are facts, after all. Yes, lots of people with similar interests dying at the age of 27 is strange. But it's still a fact.

I had just a few months to go until my birthday. And I wanted more than a few measly months alive on this planet. It might be hard to believe, what with the Tories being in power, but I was always optimistic. Always dreaming of the day that the red team got back in. And if you think about it like that, I could either be content with my final few months on Earth under a Tory leadership, or, I could do everything I could to live a while longer in the hope of the country seeing the light and voting in a Labour government.

Because seriously, if you're getting repeatedly kicked up the arse while someone nicks the pennies out your pockets you don't think '*oh, what a glorious moment. I could die happy like this*' do you?

I get the socialist passion from Dad. He's a hardcore socialist. Red through and through. Mum wasn't, though. When she still lived with us, she used to say to him that neither of them needed to vote on election day because they would cancel each other out anyway. But whenever he wasn't looking, she'd 'nip to the shop' via the polling station and tick the little box next to the Conservative candidate.

When you think about it, she was always cheating on him.

According to Dad, she wasn't always a Tory. She just didn't like this guy James Callaghan who was leading the Labour party in 1976.

But she did love me. At least that's what I tell myself anyway. And that's why I get so bloody angry with her. With Mum. Because she loved me, and yet she left with another man. I was only eight years old. I needed her. Every kid needs their mum.

She held my hair back when I was sick; she accommodated my picky dietary needs (no bean juice was to be allowed within an inch of my fried egg) and she was never shy about having 'the talk'. The birds and the bees chatter started pretty much by the time I made it to infant school. I'm certain she's the reason I was the only girl in sixth form who didn't get the clap after shagging Brett Donovan. So there's definitely some good legacy there. She wasn't born bad. Maybe life did it to her. But I genuinely believed our family life was good.

Perhaps Brett Donovan knew about the 27-club all along and that's why he frantically worked his way through half the girls at high school in a rushed frenzy. He had to get a good deal of shagging in before leaving this mortal planet.

Or maybe he was just a dick.

And given he was the year above me, and I believe is still out there, rutting like a stag in a bid to bed more poor unsuspecting ladies, he must have made it past the big 2-7.

He always liked Erasure anyway. The likes of Joy Division never got a look in. Long live the legend that is Ian Curtis. Was he was 27 too?

I'd been sleeping surprisingly well given I was reading about death every night. But that Monday morning, the alarm went off before I knew it and it was back to the same old routine again. Groundhog Day at Shaw's Static Holiday Homes.

Work was dull. Again. But it's not like I had high or even mediocre expectations anymore, so that softened the blow a little. I bought the local paper to scout the jobs pages but it felt like I was just going through the motions there, too.

There're just not many openings for a girl in her mid twenties with a degree in criminology in sunny Hull. Sounds ironic really. You'd think in Hull there'd be plenty of people who could use my expertise. Specially since I can personally name all of the petty criminals that gather in The Angel on a Friday.

But I'm not sure how transferrable any of it is either. I know criminology. I know caravans. And I know sales order forms.

Perhaps I could sell holiday homes to drug dealers who wanted to start new lives when their Gibraltar drug smuggling businesses hit the rocks? I was sure there'd be a market for that. We were hardly talking Pablo Escobar league, so I reckon a Shaw's Static Holiday Home deluxe edition could suffice for a few years of heads-down.

I could just scribble my phone number on the back of the beer mats in The Angel and the business would surely fly.

Or maybe I could just read the court files in the local paper and target potential customers there? The old-timers of course. The young 'uns still have chance to reform.

Hardcore petty criminals might need to go further than a caravan park in Withernsea if they want to protect their liberty though. Blackpool, perhaps?

I mostly spent the afternoon dreaming up business plans that were never going to happen. I was relieved when the much anticipated time of 5.30pm finally came around. Not that it marked the beginning of a night of chaos and debauchery of course. In fact, I had a nice, albeit rather boring, night in front of the telly with our Trev. After walkies, naturally.

I stopped at the supermarket on the way home and picked up a Lean Cuisine ready meal and a half-decent bottle of wine. A respectable, almost healthy, shopping basket.

Tonight was going to be a wholesome, clean pampering night. I was going to wash those toxins – and rock 'n' roll – right out of my hair.

I ran a Body Shop bubble bath, took a glass of Chardonnay into the bathroom with me and felt like if I continued to live like this, I could just about get away with hitting 30. This was the road to middle age and I was going to happily embrace it.

And to keep me company, I shoved a few batteries in my ghetto blaster and played some Paul Simon as I soaked up the bubbles and calm.

Face pack on, legs clean shaven, I treated my hair by leaving the Salon Selectives conditioner in for longer than it said on the bottle.

Then it suddenly occurred to me – Jim Morrison, Kristen Pfaff - they both died in the bath. And I'd heard hot baths could affect your circulation, and that's linked to your heart and…

Shit!

A wave of dizziness swept over me and my familiar chaotic heartbeat had returned once more. I felt like I might be sick.

I leapt out of the tub, grabbing a towel to put around me while my legs were shaking as though they might give way. With conditioner still slicking my hair back I started retching and wobbling. I grabbed the sink to steady myself and try to get my breathing back on track. I could feel my heart dancing to its own fucked up tune and it took my breath away once more. I undid the towel from around my chest to allow me to breathe more deeply. I stood for a few moments, breathing in, then out, until my heart began to slow and I could straighten up, feeling slightly steadier on my feet.

Once I'd managed to compose myself, at least to some extent, I gathered my towel around my waist and wandered into my bedroom, collapsing back on my bed exhausted from the anxiety, palpitations still lingering in the background, albeit more quietly now. My hair, complete with conditioner, was soaking my duvet cover and sticking to my skin in a slimy webbed mass of tentacles.

I felt as though I'd been close to the edge. Hovering over the cliff, close to tripping and falling into the abyss. Close to sliding under the water and never coming back up. Close to leaving this world for something new. Something I didn't want yet.

Nothing felt real, except this intense feeling of dread and darkness that hit me. That was real alright. I'd been here before. Years ago, when I was a kid. I remember this feeling. I remember feeling like this when Mum left. I remember feeling like this when I first went to uni. What the hell was it?

As my breathing began to slow, I sat up and wandered into the bathroom. I stuck my head under the sink taps and washed the conditioner away. That was a pretty intensive, albeit unintended, hair mask I'd treated myself to.

I was feeling a bit more myself, although still a little shaken by how faint and wobbly I had been. Perhaps it was my blood pressure or something? I'd always had heavy periods, maybe it was a sign of something like anaemia. Although that wouldn't account for why I felt like this as a kid. The wobbles, as I called them, had been intermittent through the years.

I decided there were to be no more bubble baths. I was going to rely on the dodgy shower attachment from now on to get clean.

I dried off and pulled on a fresh pair of pyjamas.

After the bath drama, I decided that I wasn't going to think about rock 'n' roll any more tonight. No more reading. Soap suds in the bath, soap operas on the telly.

The soaps didn't really instil a sense of innocence and clean living however. In EastEnders, Steve caught his girlfriend in bed with another woman, and in Coronation Street, Ken Barlow got another woman preggers while Dierdre'd been away looking after her sick mother.

Is life *really* like this? Affairs, bad news, murders. If I'm honest, I kind of grew up with that, so I guess, aside from the murders, the soaps aren't far off. There was a lot of swinging going on in our street when I was young.

We had pampas grass in our garden when I was a kid. I never really understood the significance of it back then. It was only as an adult that I learned it was a sign…a sign that we were open for business…as swingers.

Personally, I always loved the pampas grass. It looked like a bundle of feather dusters balancing gently on top of spiky green stems. It was so tall it constantly danced and waved at us while we were having our tea on our laps in the front room. I used to fool myself into believing that it danced along to whatever was happening on *Come Dancing* or *Top of the Pops*. I was too young to watch the affairs on Corrie back then.

It was only when Dad found out about Mum's affair that he concluded why she might have been so keen for that particular plant to go out the front. Personally, I think she just liked it.

Whatever the reason, pampas grass is still a swear word in our house.

I'll never forget my dad storming out into the pissing rain with a shovel and digging the whole thing out.

'Why have you dug a big muddy hole in the lawn, Daddy?'

'That bloody plant was toxic' he muttered. Then he stormed into the kitchen without wiping his boots, raindrops still dripping from his nose, and downed a whiskey.

He got through a lot of that stuff back then.

For years I told all my friends not to go near pampas

grass because it was as poisonous as arsenic. It was my very own version of *The Day of the Triffids*. I went from enjoying watching it dance in the breeze to being completely and utterly terrified of the stuff. It taunted me whenever I walked past it in someone's front garden. Always seemed to make Dad shudder too.

Perhaps the very public knowledge of Mum's affair was the reason why Barbara Carpenter from number 48 was trying to snog my dad under the mistletoe at my birthday party having downed one too many Babychams. Christ, that was almost eighteen years ago.

It all feels a bit sordid but maybe that's just how life is. And after all, innocence is such a naff thing, isn't it? Who wants innocence? Innocence means you've done nothing. Innocence means you're not allowed in the in-crowd to compare notes about sex and snogging and fingering and wanking. Innocence means you're nobody in a high school context. Or worse still, somebody to be picked on.

So I'm not innocent. I chucked mine away as soon as I could. And because of that, I'm full of regret.

And there's another thing I have in common with the dead. Nobody in the 27 club was indeed innocent. Nobody. Have we ever lost a 27-year-old virginal rock musician?

Innocence keeps us alive. Innocence doesn't give us the clap, or the embarrassment of the walk of shame on a Sunday morning. I threw all my innocence away. Claire's seriously overdrawn. Dave's had his moments. And now we were all in danger.

Kurt married a self-confessed teenage whore. Jim Morrison made full and proper use of the age of free love. And Janis Joplin was all about the cheap thrills.

Their talent was amazing, their fame destructive and their innocence was gone long before they were.

I decided that perhaps celibacy was the way forward. Perhaps, just like when you quit smoking and your lungs return to normal after so many years' abstinence, your virginal innocence returns to normal after abstaining from sex. The re-birth of the hymen *must* be possible. Perhaps there's a type of surgery for it?

And maybe I needed to fall in love. Maybe sex should be confined to married life only.

I wish someone had told Mum that. Although, strictly speaking, she did only have sex while married. Just not always to the man she was married to.

The following morning, I was pondering a life of celibacy as I took Trev out to the park before work.

Animals are innocent beings aren't they? Scampering around, tongue lolling out their mouths because they just don't care. They're just in life for the fun. I needed to be more Trev.

However, that was going to be a rather challenging proposition given we had a new bitch on the block…

Meet Dixie the Afghan Hound, who, apparently, is like laudanum to a Victorian poet as far as our Trev's concerned.

The pair of them, despite a significant difference in size and weight, were inseparable. Literally.

It started with a sniff. A bum sniff, sure, but in dog society that's perfectly acceptable. It's like shaking hands and saying hi.

So, to allow these young kids to suss each other's hormones and potential suitability, I politely stopped and chatted to Dixie's owner, John.

It certainly wasn't an unpleasant way to waste a little time…

Be still my racing-at-a-million-miles-an-hour heart.

He had close-cropped, very dark hair. Almost a skinhead – but not as severe. And with dark, dark brown eyes and a thin, but broad and cheeky smile. Those eyes looked so warm and sincere. What a combination. I could barely look at them for fear of blushing.

Was I blushing?

I might have been bright red, but there were no immediate

red flags with John. Often it's a case of talking those red flags down.

'Yes I know he used to be a topless waiter, Dave, but everyone has a past.'

'Yes, I know he likes Glen Madeiros, Dave, but that's surely just a minor point.'

Of course, none of those encounters went very far. Dave was always spot on with his advice. I wondered what he'd make of John…

We ended up chatting for like, ten or fifteen minutes. Turns out John had recently moved into a Victorian flat on the outskirts of the park to be closer to his job. He's a support worker, working for a supported living service for young adults with drug and alcohol problems, and he'd just been transferred from a place in Newcastle ran by the same charity.

He's a Geordie too. That accent…

I kind of skipped over what I did for a living. I harked back to my university days in a bid to impress him with my *potential*, rather than my *actual*, life.

He studied for a social work degree at Hull University. That's why he was so keen to come back and work here, he still had good mates dotted about. And it turns out we'd been to some of the same gigs at the Adelphi when I was back for the holidays in the late 80s…Pulp, Happy Mondays…

This guy was *so* on my wavelength.

I tried to impress him with my music knowledge and vinyl collection.

He talked of travelling around the country to the Trans Pennine Record Fairs in the hope of bagging a limited edition 7".

'I got some great stuff when they were in Hull City Hall. Postcard CV by the Senseless Things was a find.' I *knew* he'd be impressed.

'You're kidding me!' he said, his dark brown eyes lighting up with all the excitement of a child finally getting that glow-in-the-dark Domino Rally for Christmas.

Good God. I've met another vinyl geek. I'm not alone in this modern world of compact discs and The Spice Girls.

'No' I said, bursting with pride. 'I got their first EP there too! Love their early stuff!'

Jeeeeeeez. That's more 'vinyl cheese' than 'vinyl geek'. I always promised myself I would *never* be *that person*. The one who likes 'their early stuff' best. The one who saw them before you. The one who's never heard the pop song at number one in the charts even though they've secretly bought it from Woolworths on CD.

I lost my train of thought. Mumbled something quietly. I must have looked slightly embarrassed. He changed the subject with a warm smile, never leaving eye contact.

Those brown eyes.

'So, where's your weekend stomping ground?' he asked, and I was just about to tell him about my favourite local pub crawls (well, pub) in the hope of 'accidentally' bumping into him when I caught something that was both abhorrent and ridiculous in equal measures out the corner of my eye.

'Trevor. No!'

Nothing could relieve me from the horrifically ridiculous images that I quite simply was not prepared for. Kurt, Jim and Janis would have no problem with this. Their artistic brains had imagined and seen too much already. But I was shocked. Shocked and massively perplexed by the vision presented before me.

Dixie the Afghan Hound, the beautiful, graceful Afghan Hound with immaculate hair that's enough to rival Rapunzel's, was squatting awkwardly as Trev…

Well, let's just say they sussed each other out with a sniff and somehow came to the conclusion that they were entirely compatible.

As soon as I saw the awkward canine embrace I shot over to pull them apart but John jumped in and held me back informing me of the 'mating lock'.

It would have been dangerous to pull them apart

apparently. Their bits become intertwined. Trev becomes stuck. It's all part of the canine sex life. Apparently.

We had half the local kids on their way to school standing and jeering, the lads screaming '*go on son – give it to her*' while the girls giggled and pointed at us. And if that wasn't bad enough, we now had the excruciating task of sitting and waiting for '*around 15 – 30 minutes*' (as John informed me) until they would become 'unlocked' from one another.

Yep, apparently, it's a well-known phenomenon. When dogs mate there's no chance the fella is doing a runner straight after a one-night stand. He's stuck inside the female. Post coital cuddles are a pre-requisite. Part of the deal.

Mind, I think in my experience I've always been the one wanting to do a runner, given my poor choices which have only happened when I've ignored Dave's sound advice. But it seems Dixie, as female doggy, had no such opportunity. They were stuck together like glue.

So we stood and chatted some more. Desperately trying to ignore the intimate moment we had let the entire population of the busy morning park in on by deciding to walk our two love-struck doggies at the same time today.

I wasn't quite sure where to take the conversation after the, um, release. I knew I was going to be late for work. Again. And me and John the dogwalker never really recovered the *where-do-you-drink-cos-we-both-obviously-want-to-hook-up* conversation.

'I, um. Hope she'll be OK? I'm so, so sorry.'

Is there a law against not controlling your horny whippet in a public park?

John was a total gent about it all. If he was angry with me, he hid it rather well. Still, it wasn't a time for hanging out. I apologised again, told him how lovely it was to meet him and that maybe I'd bump into him again on the morning walk. But that next time, I'd make sure Romeo contained himself.

I rushed home, with Trevor finally on his lead, barking

commands at him rather abruptly as I couldn't hide my disappointment. Now Trevor had lost his innocence too. Christ. He was to head straight home and he was not permitted to stop and sniff. I wasn't convinced he was getting his daily *Smacko* treat today either. Especially not after seeing the mess he made on the doorstep as I was trying to find my house keys.

Oh Trevor, sex and diarrhoea, what a terrible combination. And I hadn't even had my breakfast yet.

After leaving him at home, I jumped on the packed-out bus, the blueberry Pop Tart filling still burning my mouth after I had wolfed it down at warp speed before paying the driver. I stood hanging onto the rail and feeling uncomfortably close to a dodgy looking bloke whose fingers were adorned with several oversized sovereign rings and whose torso was hidden deep below an oversized puffer jacket. Still, at least I'd have a soft landing if we crashed.

Regardless, I felt my anxiety rise every time someone else flagged the bus down, fumbled around in their pockets or handbag for-seemingly-ever in search of the final pieces of copper they needed to get from A to B, and adding another intolerable length of time to my journey. I was so late. What was I going to tell the boss this time? This one's even more ridiculous than 'the dog ate my homework'.

'Sorry I'm late, my dog was stuck in a post-coital lock with an Afghan Hound.'

It was the kind of nonsense you'd write in the late book at school, alongside '*the bus got hijacked by aliens*' or '*School's a pile of wank*'.

I decided to tell Mike I'd simply missed the bus. He'd heard that one before and seemingly accepted it.

But canine porn and doggy diarrhoea aside, really, who cared? I got to meet a wonderful man. I'd be more than happy to bump into those eyes again.

Of course, there wouldn't be any sex before marriage. Just, maybe, a little foreplay. That won't count, surely? I mean, I've already lost my innocence, so a diet is just as good as a fast isn't it?

I was already imagining the wedding. Dave in a bridesmaid's dress and a pair of Adidas, trying to keep Claire firmly in *her* bridesmaid's dress. There'd be no flashing at the wedding of the year. It would be a spectacular event.

My dad would be there. Proud as punch. Delivering a whiskey-fuelled speech about that time I fell off the climbing frame and ran home crying cos I'd split my 'fairy' when I landed with my legs either side of the swinging metal bar in the middle.

Fuck, that hurt. It must have been prepping me for the recurrent cystitis that I can't seem to shake off. Character-building Claire says (yep, Dad's met Claire at least once, so of course Claire knows all about the split fairy too).

My eyes were watering just thinking about it.

But if there's one thing that can get you through the monotony of the caravan industry it's the thought of a little romance. Or an eight-hour long daydream interspersed with a debate on celibacy with Claire.

'What the...no Emma. What a stupid. I can't even imagine. No, Emma. I mean, what would we have to talk about to get us through work? Why would you even think it.'

'Well, we usually talk about *your* hook ups, Claire. Mine aren't exactly regular occurrences anyway. I'm not sure I'd be missing much.'

I tried to explain my train of thought. There's too much intoxication. There's too much unhealthy stuff. There's too much shallow stuff.

Cue bad joke from Claire about needing men with more satisfying measurements. I continued in my endeavour to persuade her it was the right thing for me to do.

The sex isn't good enough to justify it. Like eating a cereal bar and realising you've wasted a load of calories on compact muesli when you could have slowly indulged in the delights of a Twix.

Sex with the right man was my Twix bar.

'I want to be wholesome again, Claire.'

'Can't you just switch to brown bread?'

I sighed.

'I just. I'm not sure I really enjoy it.'

'Try Mighty White instead then, they reckon that's halfway between white and brown.'

'The sex, Claire! I mean, I don't think I really enjoy the sex. It's dull. Or I'm too drunk. I just want to enjoy hanging out with someone. Someone I've got something in common with.'

'You've been watching too much Dynasty. You'll end up murdered or worse if you go chasing after some romantic nonsense. Dinner, flowers, we all know how that ends in the movies.'

This was pointless. Dave had talked me out of pop music. At least his trainers had anyway. And now Claire was talking me out of celibacy. Maybe I needed to switch. I'd take Claire to LA's (she practically lives there anyway) and talk celibacy with Dave, because, let's face it, of late, it was something he could relate to. Not out of choice, however.

After work, I headed off to The Angel to tell Dave all about Trevor's resurrection from a life of celibacy, and my ambition to live a life of celibacy. And at the same time, how I'd spotted the man of my dreams and had to practice my own restraint next time I went to the park. Maybe we humans should be kept on a leash in order to practice wholesome lifestyles?

I think Trev's safe to carry on though. In dog year's he's left 27 far behind. And I think that may have been his first time. He was obviously waiting for 'the one'. So, fair play to him. I'll give him a Smacko tonight.

Eat your heart out Anais Nin – your erotica might be first class and a bit weird at times, but you could never have conjured this one up.

'At least it was Trevor and Dixie at it on first encounter and not you and John.'

'Cut the snidey remarks Dave. I'm on a diet anyway. I'm going celibate. I'm re-building my innocence until I know I've met 'the one'.'

'Fuck me, Emma.'

Did he realise the irony of that statement? Ugh, that doesn't bear thinking about. We had to be put in the bath together as kids after falling in a slurry pit. Sex would never enter our world. Except for when we were talking about other people.

He still couldn't seem to grasp my newfound desire for a healthy lifestyle. And he was equally unconvinced that a man who must have studied the Observer's book of dogs before carefully choosing the stylish Afghan breed would be the right man for me.

'I've heard about people cutting back on stuff when they turn 40. But you're only 26. You've got years of sex, smoking and Sambuca to contend with. Live dangerously, Emma. And why an Afghan anyway? Why would a bloke choose an Afghan? Fucking weird.'

'Afghans are…highly presentable dogs, Dave. And living dangerously is the last thing I want to do. That's precisely what leads to an early death.'

'You are not joining the 27 Club Emma. Jesus. You're seriously starting to worry me with all this. You've got some unresolved issues, that's the problem. Not your age.'

'Don't be silly. I don't have issues for fuck's sake. I'm just trying to get fit and healthy. And why the hell not. That rock 'n' roll lifestyle is really not good for you. Kurt Cobain proved that. It hurts the soul.'

'You do realise that the genre of music has nothing to do with it. You're just as likely to find a glue-sniffer in LAs as you are down a dodgy alleyway. Tribes might have music in common, but our taste in music doesn't make us all exactly the same, you know.'

'Whatever'.

'And besides. It wasn't rock music that killed Kurt

Cobain. It was bringing punk rock to the masses. It was the fame. It was the immense pressure. It was becoming popular. Therefore, you could argue, that it was in fact pop music that killed him.'

It was an interesting idea, but Kristen Pfaff hadn't been so much in the public eye. And she succumbed to death.

I explained to him that it didn't matter either way. Because I was too old for clubbing full stop. So whether it was LA's or Spiders, I would no longer be out dancing through the night until the early hours of the morning.

And besides, if I wanted to lead a celibate-until-marriage kind of lifestyle, getting drunk in nightclubs was not going to be conducive.

Dave understood the idea of being more cautious and choosy regarding men, though. He'd seen me upset before, after all. And he no longer had a trombone to bash anyone over the head with like he did at school.

It wouldn't really make much difference anyway. If you don't meet the right people, you rarely have sober sex, so would I really be missing out on anything? I could barely remember those fumbles in the dark.

Don't get me wrong, I wasn't at it like a rabbit or anything. Far from it. It's just, whenever it *did* happen, it never led anywhere. I was doing it the wrong way around. Not the actual sex, but the order of talking and actual sex. Drunken sex is rarely adventurous in the karma sutra kind of way. Basically, it's rutting.

But there's something about having sex with a person just once that kind of makes you feel like you've not given too much away. I know how that sounds – you've given your body away. But if you have no expectations, nobody can cheat on you. Nobody can fool you.

Dad had expectations – he exchanged those expectations when he exchanged his vows with Mum. I wondered if it was just the once with Mum. Or whether she and her fancy man were at it for months behind Dad's back. Obviously, they knew each other for months. They never took it in turns to do the dance class drop offs and pick-ups. What *were* they doing in that hour whilst I was practicing the latest disco moves in a sequinned flared all-in-one?

Ugh.

It always upset me that she never wanted to stay and watch the class. She did the first few times. But never again.

Did they talk in that hour? Share an ice-cream? Go for coffee? Debate politics?

Or did they just shag each other's brains out?

Why couldn't she just be happy with Dad? Having different political views can only make for a better debate, surely? It could only spice things up?

For me, deep down, I wanted someone to watch movies and eat pizza with on a Saturday night. I wanted someone to share my walks with Trevor with. I wanted someone to go to the beach with, sit around a campfire and drink cans of Boddingtons whilst all wrapped up under the stars of a dark November night, snuggling up close to keep warm as the sea-air whipped around our faces with frosty lashes.

At least, that was where my daydreams about John were heading. Daydreams I needed to rid myself of. He was one guy I randomly met while walking Trev. I'd never seen him before, and I'd probably never see him again. Pull yourself together, Emma.

My cynicism was starting to make me think that celibacy before marriage would be as easy as achieving a 25m swimming badge.

'So, anyway, tell me more about this John, then.' Dave asked.

And before I knew it, I'd gone straight back into the campfire daydream that was to herald the beginning of the romance of the century.

As I headed home, however, my angst-ridden mind became preoccupied with the demise of Janis Joplin. I guess, out of all the members of the 27 club, Janis was the one I could most relate to.

No – I can't sing like Aretha Franklin and no, I don't live a wild lifestyle. But like Janis, I am a woman, and a woman who was always deemed the ugly duckling growing up.

No wonder we both wanted to stand out for different reasons.

I chucked *Pearl* on the record player, skipping over the first track to launch straight into my favourite – *Cry Baby*, wishing I had a whiskey to get into the spirit of things. I had a whole boat load of vinyl from the 60s and 70s thanks to my mum. Her record collection was left in the house and when I realised Dad was close to giving it away to the Cat's Protection League shop down the road, I was having none of it.

I think I always loved Janis as a kid because of how colourful and theatrical she looked. I had similar feelings about Adam Ant and Boy George as a teenager – but Janis was something else. The feather boas in her hair, the beads and flared trousers. I remember being sent to Brownies dressed as Janis and Brown Owl wasn't overly impressed – I couldn't understand why.

I remember reading that Janis was voted 'ugliest man on campus' in college. Have you seen her? Have you heard her? There's simply *nothing* ugly about Janis. I kind of related to it though, because I was always given grief in school after Mum left. Dad wasn't especially good at doing my hair – although he did try at first – but eventually he just started asking the hairdressers to cut it short. And I didn't miss the pain of him getting lumps of my hair wrapped around his fat fingers and my little hair bobbles. Ouch.

However, it wasn't just my hair being cut short. My wardrobe wasn't regularly updated, so half-mast trousers were standard issue. I was told I looked like a boy on a daily basis.

I think that's probably where my Dr Martens, knackered old dress and cardies look came from when I think back. I never felt particularly comfortable in a pretty dress and ribbons. Not that I wanted to blend in. Far from it. I can feel far more relaxed in something a little outlandish because then it's not really me, is it, that they're staring at. It's just a look. You can hide behind a look. Did we see the pain in Janis' eyes, or did we see the feather boas?

And besides, surely anyone would feel far more comfortable being criticised for being a bit out there rather than being criticised for being dull or quiet? We often confuse being 'out there' with confidence and happiness, when in many cases, it's the exact opposite.

Anyway, from what I knew, Janis left Texas for San Francisco where she felt she fit in more - purely because not fitting in was wholly acceptable there. Which is precisely why I love Spiders nightclub so much.

That shoddy little warehouse club was my San Francisco.

As side two of Pearl came to a close with *'Get it while you can'* it made me rethink my stance on celibacy. Janis was right in so many ways. Firstly, there is too much shit going on in the world. I mean, I know that song was written in the 70s, but nothing much has changed. The papers are still full of fighting and political nonsense.

And then there's Janis herself. Thank God she did get it while she could, because she didn't have very long in which to enjoy things. Just such a shame she got the heroin when she could.

Heroin was a drug that was simply a no-go area for me and Dave. No way would we experiment. The danger was too immense. Old and recent history taught us that.

But as far as sex was concerned, perhaps celibacy was a hasty idea. Perhaps it wasn't simply about saying no to sex until marriage. And it wasn't about opening your legs for every guy you snogged in Spiders nightclub. I think she was trying to say, if there's a bloke that you actually like, as in, not someone you've decided might just do at 1:50am through very strong beer goggles, but someone you *actually* quite like in the cold light of day. Then go for it. Why the hell not? At least that was my rather convenient explanation of her lyrics.

It's a balance isn't it. You can't reclaim your innocence. Once it's gone, it's gone. But you can choose to make better choices. Don't just get *anything* while you can – get the things you actually *want* while you can.

But don't, whatever you do, get things from other people when you've got an amazing husband at home.

I wonder if there'll ever be another Janis? Another force of nature with an amazing soulful voice and a unique look. Another little girl blue.

I guess if there is, she'll probably die young too. Not because she would deserve an early demise. But because, from what I can gather, life's a bit shitty actually.

CHAPTER 4

I was late for work. Again. And I didn't hear the bloody end of it. The number 30 never turned up so I had to walk in the pissing rain. Deep joy.

I was kind of wishing I had told the truth last time rather than blaming it on the buses. As it sounded slightly unbelievable – blaming the buses *again*.

Mike didn't look convinced. And the cheeky git dropped a comment about too many late lock-ins. Like when have I ever been to a lock-in at The Angel on a school night anyway? He doesn't know what he's on about. Just cos he spied us on the karaoke that time completely hammered.

I guess we did murder *Especially For You* by Kylie and Jason (we were being ironic, of course), so, we do deserve at least *some* bad karma.

Mind you, if he was thinking canine 'lock-ins' he'd be a step closer to the truth.

I'm so tired of this job. And not just because of Mike being on my case and the sales wankers waltzing through the office in their crappy aftershave with their crappy one-liners.

Today, for example, I must have spent at least two hours faxing papers to place orders for…I don't even know what for. Caravan bathrooms, I think. I had more fun litter picking on detention at school while my classmates jeered.

Claire was on form though…I still can't decide if she's a bit ditzy or just often too distracted to concentrate on what she's doing or saying work-wise, but my God you couldn't make some of it up.

'Mike ses he needs those order forms back that you're faxing, so you're gonna have to photocopy them before you send them.'

'Sorry, Claire. Why do I need to photocopy them? I'll just give them back once I've faxed them.'

'Duh. You'll 'ave faxed 'em by then to the bathroom people.'

'Eh? Do you mean he needs two copies of them?'

'No. But he needs these ones back, an' you can't give 'em back after you've faxed them.'

I was starting to think it was me, until I realised that Claire believed that when you faxed something to somebody, that actual physical piece of paper made the journey down the line as well.

She wouldn't believe me until we sent the first one, which she made me take a photocopy of 'just to be safe', and so when she saw it coming out the other side she had a look of astonishment on her face that warranted an EastEnders 'duf-duffer' cliff-hanger.

Magic.

This is what happens when your dad owns a café and gives you the chance to run it for three years straight from school. You don't have to do any of this officey shite. She was pretty adept at running said café by all accounts, but the office gadgets were a learning curve when she first started here in caravans. And they still are a bit of an enigma to her.

Claire's dad took a pretty standard burger place that was doing 'OK-ish' and stuck a load of American idol statues inside. It became *the* place to slurp milkshake. Plus, they always put American Chip Spice on your fries in there – a kind of pink salt that's synonymous with Hull these days and a winning recipe for Claire's family.

Who'd have thought a shoddy waxwork of Prince and pink salt would have all the makings of a highly successful burger chain? They went from living in the town to owning a five-bedroomed detached house in a quaint little village in the sticks.

I think it was possibly a love of, and commitment to, her father that first saw her shaking chip spice on every Hull teenager's chips on a Saturday. From there, her loyalty saw her taking on a full-time role after leaving school and she stayed there for three years before realising she needed a challenge.

So she ended up working in Hull's booming caravan industry.

But I'm so glad she's here. She gets me through the monotony of caravan admin. And I have to wonder if the reason she's so wild on a night out is because she's bored. Bored. As. Fuck. She's got way too much energy to sit in these swivel chairs day in, day out. And not wanting for anything of the material persuasion kind of leaves her without any challenges to face. So I guess she needs to make her own challenges.

It's funny that we're from two completely different backgrounds and yet we both ended up in the same place.

The only difference is, Claire's constantly seeking excitement and I'm constantly hiding away from it, seeking oblivion. Sure, I need to be challenged, I need a career with at least some form of intellectual stimulation. But given everything that's happened over the years, I've had enough drama to fill a lifetime of EastEnders' Christmas specials.

I don't want drama. I just want a bit of peace and quiet. I just want to be able to walk for the bus and it actually turn up on time. I want to be able to walk into the office, unnoticed, and just get on with my work. I want to be able to take the dog for a walk without him getting horny and making me late.

I wanted to go to dance class without Mum getting horny and screwing up our lives.

But speaking of going unnoticed, I feared that wouldn't happen. My Dad was about to rise up and revolt. He decided he was ready for a piece of the celebrity pie.

I never thought for a second that fame could come knocking on our door. But it has. Well, on Dad's door, at least.

There are two huge things in my life that were heavily influenced by my father: music, and socialism.

It was Dad who taught me how to play guitar. He loved any excuse to harp on about his days as lead guitarist in his psychedelic band, *The Cliff-Hangers*. The name was apparently to do with some legendary story about the drummer almost falling to his death from a steep cliff face in Filey. Luckily, he was saved by a passer-by as he was hanging on by his finger nails, watching his life flash before him.

I think they maybe did too many drugs. I'm not convinced it happened in quite that way. I think it was more a myth than a legend and it certainly didn't propel them to stardom anyway. Which is probably why Dad ended up working in a fish processing factory in West Hull. And we should probably all be incredibly grateful – if *The Cliff-Hangers* had made the big time, my wonderful father might have been another casualty of the 27 club.

I got my first guitar – a half-size electric - for my 10th birthday. My first masterpiece was *Catch the Wind* by Donovan Leitch. It took a while to get used to, but my much-anticipated gift came complete with Hal Leonard's '*Teach Yourself Guitar*' volume 1, so I had all the tools I needed. Dad said no way was he teaching me with a kid's guitar book. It'd be a crime, he said, to play *Ba Ba Black Sheep* on a Fender. So, I learned songs by Donovan and Dylan and Cohen. Which, Dad said, is why he couldn't get his head round the fact I liked to listen to '*some guy with messy hair screaming about paranoia*' when I'd had '*such a good musical education.*'

I swear parents only dislike their kids' music because they can't lay claim to discovering it first. Everyone's snobby about their own music taste.

So I never made it into a rock band and I never made the pages of Melody Maker. But Dad, however, was about to become Hull's answer to Che Guevara. He was about to earn some fame in a completely different way…

Onto my dad's second influential topic – social justice. Dad always encouraged my non-existent career in criminology. Being a socialist, he wanted the right people working in the justice system. That's what he said, anyway. I was at least hopeful he didn't want me passing insider knowledge onto the locals in The Angel. Nah, Dad's involvement with them lot only went as far as buying the odd packet of illegally imported ciggies.

He was always quite the activist in his younger years. But since Mum had the affair, he's just been really, well, depressed I guess. He puts the world to rights when he's had a whiskey, but I don't think he's been out on a march in years. And it's been even worse since he lost his job at the fish factory.

Me and Dave have always been mindful to get him out to the pub – but we've also been mindful to watch how many return trips he makes to the bar. I know he sneaks a cheeky snifter when we're not looking and returns with a pint pretending that's all he bought.

It's amazing how one person can have such an impact on your whole being. Mum cheating on him, it just meant he was never the same. He was so conflicted between anger and sadness it left him in a kind of limbo. Kind of like the undead. He just floated about the house, drinking tea, watching telly and eating peanuts.

And watering that bloody lilac plant as if it would magically bring his cheating wife back home.

Me and Trev were round at his again for our morning cuppa. But he seemed happier than usual. I say happier - he was positively buzzing. That's not a state I've seen Dad in for a long time.

I cooked our Sunday dinner, which I often try to do as an excuse to go round. Try being the operative word. I bought a chicken to roast in the oven, boiled up some spuds then bashed them around the pan to fluff them up before roasting them with the chicken. That was one of Mum's tricks. I mixed up a Yorkshire pudding mix, threw it in a hot muffin tray bubbling and spitting with vegetable oil, and microwaved some veg. The gravy, however, was going to be Bisto's best. I always quite enjoyed the cooking, no matter how it turned out, and turned Radio 1 on to accompany me in the kitchen – much to Dad's disgust.

Dad still pretends my Yorkshire puddings are the business, even though I know they're as flat as a fart. He's done it ever since I was little. We both know they're like frazzled, bowl-shaped crisps, and that they add nothing to the meal except the need for extra gravy, but we both play along regardless. It brings us some sense of comfort.

Mum's Yorkie's simply *were* the business. Always perfectly fluffed up into imperfect fluffy mis-shapes. Dave was usually present for dinner back then - I don't think his family really did round-the-table family dinners. It was always a tray in front of the telly at theirs. And often all at different times.

He became like part of the family – and given Mum and Dad never gave me a brother or sister, I was always grateful for his presence.

It's easy to look back with rose-tinted glasses, though, isn't it? Remembering the love and the fun times and the competitiveness that poured out of us all when *Name That Tune* was on the telly. But when I think about it, just like her Yorkshire puddings, Mum certainly wasn't perfect.

And I found it hard not to blame myself. I nagged and nagged to start that disco dance class. But that's where they met. Waiting for us kids at the end of class; ferrying us from one dance competition to another in cheap sequinned leotards (us, not them), and treating us to post-class McDonald's meal deals.

They had plenty of time to chat or…whatever. Dad thought he was onto a winner getting his Saturday mornings to himself. And me, I was unwittingly aiding and abetting an affair. If it wasn't for me, she'd never have met him.

But, let's remember the positives, she did a mean roast dinner. So me and Dad always tried to keep that going. To keep what was left of our broken family together.

It felt like yesterday, and yet, since she left us, so much has happened.

1. I graduated with a degree in Criminology.
2. I lost my virginity
3. I lost a rock icon.

And some things didn't change in all those years:

1. My Yorkshire puddings never improved
2. The loos in The Angel never got that refurb
3. Dad never stopped pining after Mum

I plated up the dinner and made a little bowl of leftovers for Trev to snaffle in the kitchen. We sat round the table but had the telly on in the lounge whilst we ate. It was tradition.

I rounded it off with Viennetta ice-cream and, before allowing our calorie-ridden bodies to snooze in the lounge, we decided to take Trev out for a walk, with Dad driving us all to the coast for a change of scenery. He had news to tell me, he said. Hopefully it would explain the strange hyper mood he was in. Seeing Dad smiling so much unnerved me. I thought he must have robbed a bank. Perhaps my criminology career was about to start here and now.

We drove to Fraisthorpe beach, barely speaking. Dad seemed distracted but happy, singing along loudly to his Clash album, asking me to rewind the tape after *I Fought The Law* played so he could sing his favourite song over and over again.

We got out the car and walked through the prickly sand dunes and onto the beach. The water was rough and choppy. A cold North Sea. It might be summer but the North had a reputation to uphold. It didn't let us down.

Trev returned the soggy tennis ball we threw for him and Dad scooped it up, chucked it back towards the sea and wiped his hands on his jeans before taking a deep breath and turning to me, excitement lighting up his eyes.

'You alright Dad?' I asked as he stood in front of me, his hands on my arms, looking me straight in the eyes.

'I just got this letter through the door, Emma. I had no idea I had applied. I can't believe it.'

He let go of my arms, stood up straight and took in about ten lungfuls of sea air whilst looking up to the clouds, his chest puffed outwards and his face full of pride.

Crikey. He's lost it. I felt a wave of familiar panic rush over me. What the hell had he done? Was he going to leave us too?

'What letter? What have you applied for? Or not? Sorry, Dad, rewind a bit will you...' I could feel that strange sensation in my face. Pins and needles. And my breathing was beginning to get faster and shallower. God, it was me who was in desperate need of ten lungfuls of sea air right now.

'I was mortified.' He continued. 'Then, when I thought about it, I thought, you can't just complain about the government, you have to take action. It was a wake-up call Emma. I have a role to play in society.'

'Dad. Sorry, I've no idea what you're talking about. Are you running for counsellor?'

'Counsellor? Jesus, Emma. What do you take me for?'

'Well, I don't know. I mean, you're not exactly yourself right now. I've no idea what you've gotten into and, frankly, Dad, I'm worried about you.'

I felt my throat tighten up. I was struggling to swallow. My brain was pleading with him to spit it out and get it over with.

'There's no need to be worried, love. This is where it all starts.'

'Where what all starts, Dad, just tell me, please.'

'Me and Bob. We're going to thrash the bastards, Emma.'

'You're not going to watch Grimsby play again are you Dad?'

'No, Emma. We're going on BBC Question Time.'

My shoulders dropped about three feet and I burst out laughing. He wasn't impressed. In fact, he looked positively crushed.

'What's so funny? Think I can't do it?'

'No, Dad. It's not that at all. Course you can do it. I just. I thought you might be leaving town or committing a crime or something. I'm just. Well. Relieved, I guess. Good on you Dad. I'm proud of you, I really am!'

With that I grabbed the daft lump and hugged him close. Of course he wasn't going to leave us! We were a family. I felt terrible that I had doubted him. But I'd had no idea Dad and Bob were dreaming of being political TV stars.

In fact, I don't think he had any idea either. They apparently applied from the safety of The Angel and its luxurious metaphorical beer duvet after a few too many.

The pair of dopes!

I'd never seen Dad so passionate and enthused about anything. Not since Mum left us. He had a sparkle in his eye – albeit a mischievous one – but a sparkle is a sparkle. He was alive again.

I was so, *so* pleased for him. We continued the walk on the beach with Dad talking about what he could finally say to which MP and why, jabbing his finger into the air in front of us as if he was in the moment.

He told me all about the numerous 'planning meetings' that he had arranged with Bob in the run-up to the big political show hitting Hull University's student union hall next month. So, his social diary was on the up too. Or at least, he was about to be spending a lot more time in The Angel - and their takings would be on the up.

We jumped in the car and headed back, chattering non-stop about the state of today's government, the changes we needed to see and the biased spend that never made its way to the good people of Hull. The bastards.

Dad was so fired up it was lovely. When we pulled into his street and parked up, he walked a little way with me and Trev towards mine so he could pass the newsagent – he needed to stock up on his 'research materials' – namely The Guardian and Viz magazine.

I gave him a big hug and we went our separate ways, both with a spring in our step, feeling that, finally, something was going our way. And Dad, more than anyone I knew, deserved a little happiness. His happiness levels had been bankrupt for years.

I was just enjoying the familiar walk and sense of homeliness when, bam, it hit me - that impending sense of doom. That feeling you get when you think everything's actually going well and then it hits you. That's not normal. That's not what happens. This isn't all it seems…

My brain started racing with thoughts about civil unrest and Dad's arrest. Oh God, what if this really could spell the final break up of our family? What if he was thrown in prison for throwing a punch to the face of the Prime Minister? What if he became a target for right-wing terrorists? What if, what if, what if…?

Maybe my turning 27 wasn't just a threat to me, maybe it was a threat to anyone close to me? Maybe it was a threat to my Dad? Should he really be putting himself out there in this way? I was panicked for his safety. I couldn't lose him, not after everything. Not my Dad.

Everything was beginning to feel like a threat. My impending birthday. Dad's TV appearance. Oh God, and what about Trev? I've got to stop leaving him alone in the house at night. What if someone broke in and harmed him?

My fingers began to tingle, and I felt an overwhelming rush of blood away from the head. Argh this couldn't happen now! I was walking along the street. Jesus, not now.

My thoughts were getting increasingly faster and increasingly blacker. But the only way to deal with them was to live through these risky events. I was holding on for dear life. For everyone's dear life.

How could I possibly protect us all? My breathing began to speed up, and I felt claustrophobic. Yet I was out in the open air.

Trev seemed oblivious. I looked at him and felt jealous. Jealous for his innocent joy.

All of a sudden it became too much. My legs buckled and I fell to the ground, feeling my hands smart and graze as they hit the gravelly pavement. My vision was blurred and my heart was pounding. I could see vague movements going past me, cars, people, all floating past like fuzzy blobs. They probably thought I was drunk.

In the confusion I'd dropped Trev's lead. But he was right here with me. He hadn't run off and was happily licking my hand as I picked it up to review the stony damage. His wet nose was nudging my face and he was whining a little.

Then I felt a hand on my shoulder.

'Alright Emma, my love?'

I looked up and, as my eyes adjusted and my breathing slowed, I made out a familiar figure.

It was Doreen. I'd never seen her in daylight before, but it was her alright. I recognised the trainers.

'Oh, hi. What are you doing here?'

She took me by the arm and helped me to my feet.

'You're alright lovey. I've got you.'

We linked arms and walked slowly down the road together, Doreen taking Trev's lead.

I felt a bit spacey and drained. Not to mention really stupid and embarrassed. What the hell just happened?

'I must be low on blood sugar or iron or something. Felt really out of it there.'

'You don't need to be embarrassed you know, love.'

'What do you mean?'

'You've been through a lot over the years. You're bound to feel anxious.'

'I'm not anxious. I just went faint, that's all.'

I reassured Doreen that I was more than capable of walking through the ten-foot and back to my house. She passed me Trev's lead, said she'd see me in the Angel and continued towards her little house. It was beautifully decorated with a pristine garden – which I have to say always surprised me given how much time Doreen spent propping up the bar.

As a new week came around, I reverted back to the usual route for the morning walk. Me and Trev had a nice, chilled stroll, taking our time. It was Bank Holiday. I still got up at the same time as usual, just in case John the dogwalker was out and about with Dixie.

As much as work can be a boring pain in the arse, holidays with nowt planned can be even worse. At least with work you know you're not *supposed* to be enjoying it. Sadly, John wasn't in the park to brighten up my day. *And* it started to piss it down. So I made a trip to the Apollo video shop.

There's nothing to do during the daytime in Hull when the weather's bad. And given the time of year it really should have been warmer. But I think the weather Gods forget to send the sunshine up North. Maybe they're like those Southerners that don't think anything exists north of the Thames, so they forget about us. Thank God Santa Claus didn't.

Due to the recent grey and rainy weather and the fact you can't spend every single night in the pub, I'd literally been flitting between movie genres depending on my mood. I could go from *Pulp Fiction* to *The Lion King* in one fell swoop.

However, I could not go from The Lion King to porn in one fell swoop. Or in any kind of longer-term swoop for that matter.

Jesus Christ. My face must have been beetroot.

'Ms Barclay. Before we can let you take out Free Willy, we need to ask that you pay the late fee for 9 Lives of a Wet Pussy.'

What the actual fuck? She caught me off guard there…

'Sorry, what was that?'

'You're, um…husband is it? He took out 9 Lives of a Wet Pussy and returned it three days late'

'Sorry, you must be mistaken…'

'No, Ms Barclay. It says here, Mr Barclay owes £1.75 in late fees for 9 Lives of a Wet…'

'OK – can you stop saying that please. I've got the picture.'

I was frantically trying to find some silver in my purse when…

'I'd like to see you in that picture' – it was a goading voice behind me. Some nasty little scrote in a tracksuit. No more than 17. Surrounded by two more little scrotes giggling like Dastardly and Muttley.

I rolled my eyes and let out an audible sigh.

'Oh, would you.' I snapped.

Jesus was that the best I could do?

'Ha she's gone red mate. She's desperate for a seein' to.' Scrote number had two joined in now.

'D'you want to both fuck off…wankers.'

Again, another lame response. Why had I never banked a clever riposte or two for times like this…

I turned to the shop assistant who somehow managed to look smug despite an obvious lack of any other emotion, and I slammed some coins on the desk in front of her. 'Here's your late fee. You can keep Free Willy!'

I turned on my heel in a whirlwind of cringe, anger and a bucketload more cringe as Kappa-clad kid number one piped up again…

'I've got a free w…'

This time it was the finger. You can't go wrong with a finger. More respect to me. And then…

'Swivel on that.'

I was doing so well with just the finger. No commentary was required, damnit.

I'll have to join Blockbuster's now 'cause there's no way I'm going back in there.

I'll bloody kill Dad for this! Porn! Fuck's sake! On my card!

Walking down the street I must have looked frantic trying to shake those images out of my head. My poor, poor mind. It was fragile enough without this.

If I needed to have a window into my dad's sex life, it could at least have been through stained glass. This picture was all too clear. I knew what he was watching...

9 lives of a

Wet...

Pussy...

Scrote...

Willy...

Stain!

Gah!

There were too many undeniably very wrong words whirring round my head.

Good God. Come on. Shake the demon sex thoughts away.

I ditched the movie night idea and headed to The Angel. Back in the pub. It wasn't intended and I had tried my best to do something a little healthier but that got far too dirty, far too quickly. I took Trev with me that night – he was a hit with the locals, and I was keen to keep him close by. I hated leaving him alone in the house – even more so recently.

I sat down with Dave, while Trev wandered around the bar getting attention from everyone, and told him about my embarrassing Apollo video shop debacle. I swear Dave was close to pissing his pants with laughter.

'He's waking up, Emma. He's been in some kind of deep depression since, you know...I'm pleased for him'.

'Are you kidding, Dave? Pleased? I'm horrified. My mind will never be able to wander freely without bumping into that…image again.'

Dave explained to me that sex was a basic human requirement and I needed to give Dad a break; that just because I was thinking of giving up casual sex didn't mean Dad had to stop living his life to the full.

Every sentence in the conversation made me shudder.

'Can we change the subject please?' I begged.

It really wasn't doing me any good trying to empathise with my dad's sexual needs. I never knew he had any.

'OK. So tell me about this Question Time business then'.

I told Dave all about Dad and Bob's quest to get Hull on the political map. Dave was smiling throughout. He said he was pleased for Dad, and that it was about time he started living again. And that porn and politics were obviously the key ingredients missing from his life.

There was only three weeks to go 'til the TV cameras would be zooming in on Dad, Bob and their pre-prepared questions. Dad was throwing a few ideas around. None of which I was particularly comfortable with. One of which I was convinced would have him immediately removed from the studio.

The unsuspecting panellists were to include Edwina Curry, Ian Hislop and Hull's very own John Prescott.

His first suggested question was:

'John. What hope could the Labour party offer to the working class of Hull, many of who are struggling to find work during this bleak Tory reign?'

So far so standard for Question Time…

He also contemplated:

'I'd like to ask Edwina about her new book, A Parliamentary Affair. Is it really an autobiography and if so, have you remained a true blue?'

Not sure why that one was so important to him, but then again, I had no idea he would nick my Apollo card to binge on porn. I guess people can surprise you. Or perhaps he was just concerned about the blues infecting the reds. After all, Ms Curry did have a particular obsession with salmonella – and that sounded about as healthy as her politics.

Of course, Dad's not a fan of extra-marital affairs, so this exposé was another good reason for him to hate on a Tory.

Regardless of the political banter, I was beginning to feel fidgety. Nirvana came on the jukebox and all I could think about was darkness, so I stuck a load of coins in to change the record. When I heard Kurt Cobain's voice I was consumed by the idea of pain and death. Like a constant edge of dread was clouding over me, triggered by his beautiful voice. A double-edged sword.

'Jesus, Emma. Simply Red?'

Our friendly bucket hat-clad drug dealer was standing behind me as I accidentally teed up a pop ballad.

'I want some Oasis on. What you playing at? You need some drugs, girl. Get you back to normal'

Fair do's, a little something might have helped to take my mind off Dad's…R&R. But, nope, not tonight. Drugs don't mix well with people my age.

'Nah, mate. I've given up. Bad for your soul that stuff.'

'Right Emma, OK. I'd argue that Simply Red's bad for your soul but you're obviously going through some kind of crisis so…'

'I'm not. Quite the contrary. I'm tuning into my wellbeing, actually.'

The conversation continued with me getting grief for drinking pints of lager and smoking ciggies and how the only thing making drugs worse for my health the prospect of a spell inside. Decent sales tactic I guessed.

'We're defined by manmade laws, Emma. We need to break free and see life as it really is. Without the constraints that we've made for ourselves. We're like Marley in his chains, Emma. We need to loosen things up.'

Yep, the guy had definitely had a smoke that night. I made my excuses and headed back to the table.

'So, back to your dad's sexual resurrecti…'

'Dave please!'

I stood up to order another round. I needed releasing from the horrific realisation that both my dad and my whippet were actively rampant. Could I ever look at them in the same light again?

Perhaps I was jealous?

When I got to the bar Brenda was buzzing. The idea of 'her Bob' making it on the small screen for Question Time was seemingly the most hotly anticipated event since the Berlin Wall came down.

'We need a pub screening.' She announced while expertly tilting the second pint glass to finish my order. 'We've got two of our own on there. Fighting for our rights. Speaking out. Heading to the frontline like Hull's soldiers. They deserve nothing less than the England squad. The big screen's coming out!'

It was heartening seeing the local community getting behind the big event. There was even a poster designed, with dreadful clip art featuring images that had nothing to do with politics (except for the occasional egg, in honour of the salmonella scare queen), for the main event.

Yes, Dad and Bob were real life celebrities. Even *I* felt like a celebrity. Just when I was trying, at all costs, to keep myself out of the spotlight and safe from all things rock 'n' roll.

'Nice one, Emma.'

'You must be so proud, Emma.'

Some of the punters just gave me an appreciative nod as the news had spread like wildfire thanks to the dodgy posters.

And as proud as punch that I was, I just couldn't shake the dread. This was going to be a big event. It was big news. I just didn't want it to change things.

Dad was in his late forties, so he'd got well past the age of 27 and barely had a scratch on him in all those years. But I started to wonder if the media had missed something. They were latching onto the fact that so many rock stars died aged 27, but what if there were many more, under-reported tragedies linked to the number. How many rocks stars' parents or siblings died when they hit 27? What if all of us, rock stars or not, had something terrible happen when we turned 27, and we just never made the link?

And what if Question Time was to make him famous? Fame doesn't seem like a particularly healthy status to have, given what we know. And people turn on you. What if people turned on Dad and Bob?

Fame brings you to the masses and leaves you exposed. Whether people agree with you or not, they're going to comment, they're going to hold your every thought, quote and action under the spotlight and scrutinise it. My God, the pressure.

And regardless of who supports you when you're on your way up, a struggling nobody trying to be somebody, as soon as you've got a platform, as soon as you're somebody, you're not like your supporters anymore, so your supporters distance themselves.

It seems so very British, despising someone for their success.

Was it the pressure of fame that took Kurt?

I really couldn't understand why we all dreamt of fame anyway. Because when you think about it, all fame is, is people knowing your business. It's like getting too drunk in The Angel and announcing your most sordid secrets to the world.

One minute, you're this cool twenty-something in Adidas drinking a pint with an air of authority. The next, you've told the entire pub that you once had a wank while watching Penelope Keith on the telly and your mum walked in on you and dropped your tea all over your bedroom carpet in shock. What a mess. It was a lasagne ready meal.

You also went on to inform them that you then couldn't get the image of your mother out of your head whenever you were trying to 'relax'.

You are no longer that cool teenager in the trainers. You're a berk.

True story, that. Poor Dave. He really shouldn't drink Drambuie. It loosens the lips.

Perhaps fame is the act of selling yourself to the Devil. Perhaps it's not about the talent at all. It's all about the fame. I mean, Bucks Fizz were famous. Although they're still alive…so that's screwed that theory up. But they're pop music. And fame is more relevant to death in rock 'n' roll. And socialism is certainly more rock 'n' roll than it is pop. Especially when the Tories are in power. Because your views can only be seen as rebellion. I reckon the soundtrack to the Tories would be something poppy performed by some geezer in a trendy suit.

The Labour party would have Senseless Things to mark their re-election. I was certain of it.

'Emma. Oi. Emma. You listening or what? Jesus, you're away with the fairies. Hope you're not obsessing about Kurt Cobain again?'

'Soz Dave.'

I was still wondering if Dad's upcoming appearance could have disastrous repercussions. My hands started to tingle again.

'Another pint please, Bren'.

CHAPTER 5

Why did I do it? It's so bad for me. Just because Dave can handle a bit of the naughty stuff it doesn't mean I should follow suit. If I have two Diet Cokes I'm on a one-way trip to panic central. Cocaine? Ten minutes of fun followed by ten hours of shit.

I caved in. What a dick. A little bit of grief from bucket-hat-man, a few too many pints and…

My nose had been itching like there was a bad bout of chickenpox breaking out in one of the nostrils and my heart was racing like a greyhound clumsily taking on the occasional show jump obstacle.

There was no alternative. It was going to be a duvet day. The boss was therefore informed of my terrible 'period pain'. Men never argue with that do they?

And it was still going when I finally surfaced around 6pm after tossing and turning for hours in bed but not having the courage to actually emerge into the cold light of day.

I was all set to watch Blossom and eat a frozen pizza but my ticker started massively kicking off again. It was like it was trying to have a second innings of coke-fuelled fun but missing out the 'fun' part. It was like it was too drunk to dance but was trying anyway, missing the beat, fucking up the rhythm, going way faster than the DJ.

And the MC was shouting: – 'Heart attack posse in the house. Let me hear you screeeeeeeeeeeam.'

I wanted to scream.

If that fucking whistle blows, we all know what's next. Time out for Emma. But it was too early. It was still weeks, months even, until my 27th birthday. 26 wasn't a year to go. My logic didn't stop me feeling petrified though.

Maybe some of us can't help ourselves. We've a certain fate assigned to us from birth and our behaviours just act out until we reach it.

Taking drugs makes me feel tainted and dirty and shameful because I've pumped my innocent being with chemicals and alcohol and tar. And I wake up with that whole 'what the hell was I talking about last night', 'who was I telling it to' and 'ah shit, did I ask a club doorman if he was bullied in high school again?'; narrative that just won't let you fall back into the unconscious state you can only dream of. If you could dream, that is, but your brain won't let you.

So you call everyone you came to within half a mile of that night to ascertain whether you did, in fact, put the final doornail in your already miniscule social abilities coffin?

(everyone being Dad and Dave).

And the panic - it's the worst. Never again.

All this stuff adds up. Drugs and alcohol.

Why did Jim Morrison suffer a cardiac arrest? Why did Jimi Hendrix suffer asphyxiation?

I was on my own with my heart doing backflips as I tried to keep calm on the sofa, Trev watching me with his head tilted to one side, looking mightily confused. When I was little, I always turned to Mum when I was scared of something. And impending death was definitely something she would have allowed me to interrupt Corrie for.

Mum, I've had a nightmare.

Mum, I feel sick.

She'd hold the duvet up as a signal for me to climb in, she'd put her arm around me and I'd immediately fall back to sleep, feeling safe and warm. Not even Dad's snoring from the other side of the bed could stir me when I was in Mum's safe little cocoon of love.

Somehow, these nice memories just make things worse.

The post-cocaine panic did eventually calm down. But I had to take Trev round to Dad's just to make sure I was with someone who was able to dial 999 in case I keeled over and snuffed it.

The things we think are a good idea when we've had a bevvy too many. So that's the problem? Have I ever taken drugs when sober? No. Of course not.

And on top of the chemical hangover, I had to deal with Trev's little accident. He managed to shit all over the floor. Again. And he only just missed my special edition copy of Melody Maker (RIP Kurt.) with his Pedigree Chum spatter.

What the fuck do they put in that stuff?

(Note to self – MUST ring the vets tomorrow. This poop problem is becoming abnormal)

(Second note to self. MUST ALSO laminate that bloody magazine!)

Couldn't be arsed with cooking dinner and certainly couldn't face the public for a pub meal. So I sent Dad off to the shops for fish 'n' chips and we sat and ate them out the paper, watching Romancing the Stone on one of Dad's dodgy pirate videos.

I started to feel a bit better after all that though. The drama that our movie heroes were going through made mine pale into insignificance. Either that, or it just gave me something else to focus on.

When I got home I put new sheets on the bed, dewberry oil on my skin and lil' Trevor got tucked up on the bed with me when I was ready to go to sleep.

It was a brave move. Trev sleeping on the bed isn't really a great idea right now…maybe I need to laminate my duvet as well as Melody Maker.

I woke up still feeling tired but the sun was shining and that doesn't seem to happen too much. So there was no point missing what little of it we had. I stretched my legs out to find Trev tucked up at the bottom of the bed in his spot. He stirred, circled a little then wandered over to me to snuggle up.

Sunshine or no sunshine, the whippet was not keen to move that morning.

I said the magic 'walkies' word though and all was well. He leapt up off the bed, running ahead of me and turning his head every two seconds to check I was still following him.

I stuck the kettle on and reminded myself that I was to become teetotal. Well – at least I was going to tone things down a little. I had to be realistic. And certainly no toxic drugs were to pass through my nasal passages anymore. I was just thankful I'd survived Saturday night's antics. There were to be no more of these shenanigans. So I'd better buy bigger cartons of milk to support the change in my night time regime.

Shots of Drambuie were to become mugs of hot tea.

Trev ate his breakfast furiously, the greedy blighter. Pushed his bowl at least once into each corner of the kitchen.

We got out early for our quick walk (the one I promised Trev over an hour ago. Bad parent), then I grabbed my work bag and strolled down to the bus stop. The bus was on time for once. And I even felt like I'd had a productive day.

Making positive life choices is obviously good for the soul.

I got through a huge stack of papers and even found Claire's night-on-the-town stories amusing. I'd left the office with an empty in-tray and an overflowing out-tray. I could tell Mike was impressed.

I also managed to get Trev an appointment with the vet after work. Given the state of his ahem…doings…that morning I thought it might be best to get him checked out.

The look on his little face when he realised we were heading into animal hell. Or the veterinary surgery as I prefer to call it.

Have to say, speaking on behalf of your dear doggy is just as difficult as speaking out about your own embarrassing ailments – I really felt for him. I could tell he was feeling embarrassed, poor little fella. He was hanging his head, his nose pointing downwards and his big eyes looking up. Bless him.

'What does it smell like?' the vet asked me about Trev's, ahem, doings.

'Well, it smells like poo'.

'But does it smell of anything in particular? It might help me understand if he has an infection.'

'Um. Yes. It smells like…. awfulness.'

Not sure how much my olfactory observations helped in the veterinary consultation, but I was asked to drop off a stool sample that week to double check things, was given some drugs for him and I was also advised to stop feeding him that revolting slop in a can (yeay). Instead, I needed to cook plain chicken breast for him for the next few weeks so that bloody whippet was going to be eating better than me!

The poor lamb apparently had something called IBS (Irritable Bowel Syndrome) which is where his gut goes into spasm and that's the cause of the diarrhoea and the need for a new carpet by all accounts. She was going to do some other tests to be sure, but she said he has all the classic signs so it's quite likely that's what we were looking at and what he needed treating for. So a new diet was on the cards.

I guessed I could just cook meals for two instead of one though; which might save some pennies and it made a nice change from them bloody Lean Cuisine ready meals.

As if being single didn't make me enough of a target for the taunts from the factory lads, it also worked out at a greater cost per head, so if I could share a meal with my little lad that had to be a good thing surely?

However, in other news…

Turned out Dixie the Afghan hadn't been too well either, because she was just coming out of the other consulting room as we were leaving. And of course that meant she was with the lovely John! I did a double take…but there was that unmistakeable Geordie accent.

'Hi, pet. Trev not well?'

'Oh hi! Yeah. He's um…. he's got this stomach thing. Dixie?'

'I think we're going to be related.'

'Sorry?'

'Birds and the bees, Emma. Dixie's with child. At least, with puppy. Or puppies even. I think I have a sneaky suspicion who the dad is…'

'Ohhh……'

'Don't worry though. She's doing well. I should have got her done. But I was kind of thinking I might breed her with another Afghan...'

'I see. But now you're going to have little Whafghans instead'.

Why do I try to be funny when I'm nervous? At least he forced a little laugh.

'Seriously though' I piped up in a bid to move away from my feeble attempt at a joke. 'Can I help? Are we supposed to like, give you maintenance money or something? A year's supply of Pedigree Chum?'

He laughed and his gorgeous cheeky smile spread across his face.

'Don't be daft, Emma, pet. See you at the park tomorrow? Not sure they can do much more damage now. No point keeping Romeo and Juliet apart anymore.'

And with a quick wink, he was away.

Fuck. Afghan crossed with Whippet. It was new, I guessed.

So the reason I hadn't seen him is because poor Dixie was up the duff, not because he'd been avoiding me. But it was business as usual from the next day (i.e. she'd be doing her business in the fresh air again).

After leaving the vets I decided that, just to be safe, I'd hit the supermarket and treat Trev to something nice, and bland, for tea. As it made sense to cook for two instead of one, we both enjoyed a meal of chicken breast and plain rice – with a side of green beans thrown on for me. It wasn't the most appetising, but at least it was clean and healthy.

The following morning, me and Trev headed out to the park in the hope of bumping into our romantic interests. I was keeping a close eye on Trev though – was he stopping to sniff some girl dog's wee on that blade of grass? Or was he about to produce more awfulness?

You don't like to rush them when they're having a good sniff. For all I knew, he could have been communicating with some long-lost uncle whippet through doggy hormones. They could have been sitting on that blade of grass for weeks, waiting for a family member to come along and breathe them in.

What is it that they're figuring out when they obsess over grass? If it's 'who's been here then?' what do they do with that information? It's like detective work. For dogs. I imagined Trev with a Columbo style mac and cigar weeding out the local doggy trouble causers.

Anyway, eventually he stopped and did his shaky legged crouch. Oh, this was not good. I just wish when you're needing to collect a canine stool sample, they could at least have the courtesy to make it a bit more solid.

Eueeww this was not going to be fun. But at least we would find out for certain if we had him on the right diet now. So perhaps I only needed to carry out this disgusting exercise once.

I managed to collect a stool sample – but I'd lost the little pot the vet gave me. I was always keen to scoop up Trev's poop so I normally had these little black bags for it. Mum always brought me up to think about the future of our planet Earth, not just what we can get out of it today. But I'd ran out of those, or left them in my other jacket pocket…or something.

So in the absence of black poopy scoop bags I had to make do with a freezer bag. It's seriously not pleasant being able to see the contents of poop bags – especially when your dog has IBS and its spattered all over individual blades of grass. Jesus.

I was crouching on the floor, my head straining backwards, desperately trying to pick up enough of Trev's doings for testing, with the poor little lad sitting beside me with his head down (I swear they feel embarrassment like we do) when I heard a familiar voice behind me.

'Morning Emma.'

I stood, quickly swinging the translucent bag of doggy IBS poop behind and wondering how long he'd been stood there.

Oh God.

'Hi John.'

'Nice to see you share my concern for the environment too!'

Shit! We were actually standing talking about poo. We hadn't even had our first drink yet, never mind anything else. Surely these sorts of conversations should be confined to three years into a steady relationship and living together? You know, when you're able to fart in front of each other without a care in the world.

'Ha ha, yeah.' I replied, desperately trying to think of a way to get the see-through freezer bag out of the gaze of his gorgeous eyes and this potentially productive conversation.

Productive. That's really not the right word right now.

I had been desperate to bump into him but collecting a stool sample was never in my daydreams about this moment. Still, our pets had already fucked each other so, you know. I guess you could say we had kind of fast-forwarded to that three-year, living together, farting in front of each other stage.

Maybe not.

I stuck my fingers through the loop of the freezer bag to free up my hands to open my rucksack and get rid of the offending matter.

There was no way it was going straight into my work bag though. I hadn't thought this through. I mean, we've all been there when packing last night's leftover chilli and it ends up leaking all over your notebook, hairbrush and Tampax.

I still had yesterday's packed lunch box with me so tried, as hard as I could, to manoeuvre it into there without him getting too much of an eyeful.

This wasn't just doggy poop. This was IBS doggy poop.

I cursed myself for forgetting to stock up on those black poop bags.

'So, um. Is Dixie doing alright? Any strange cravings to speak of. Shame she's not craving poop, it would have saved me a job.'

I was trying to be funny. I do that when I'm nervous. I'm not funny. And job was really the wrong word right now.

So. Many. Wrong. Words.

I must change the topic of conversation. This was not going well.

'Haha. She's taking it all in her stride. How's things with you?'

'Yeah, not bad. Except for the toilet troubles we're having with little Romeo over here.'

I was speaking at a rate usually reserved for a bid caller at an auction, thanks to the nerves. And the crippling embarrassment.

It was strange, as although I'm certainly no sex goddess oozing confidence, I don't usually get this nervous around men. Could this be because he's not just any man? He must be the one? And of course, nobody from the past, has ever been close to being the one.

'So. Hehe. We're going to be related then. Do you know how many pups we're expecting?' I was trying to get the conversation back on track.

'Not yet. I'll certainly let you know. We'll be regulars at the vets for a while what with the check-ups.'

My heart was fluttering. But not in a post-hangover kind of way - in a good way. I struggled to look into his eyes even though I was desperate to. Such a kind face. Such a cheeky smile. Such laid-back confidence.

Such knowledge about post-coital canine lock.

He noticed me looking away bashfully and smiled a knowing smile.

'Emma. I've got to dash. I've got an early shift today. But. I wondered...'

Here it comes.

'..I wondered if you fancied going for a drink sometime?'

It was a fairly bog-standard line. But I had never been so pleased to hear it.

'Um. Yes. Course. That'd be lovely.'

'Great. Have you got a pen on you in that bag?'

Oh deep joy. I was delving back into the bag of poo. However, this man was worth it. Luckily, it didn't take too long for me to find a biro. He scribbled down my number on an old bus ticket and promised to call. Then he was off.

Result! I was desperately trying to hide my great big grin from all the other dog walkers and kids in the park, when Trev reminded me it was time to go by pulling on his lead.

As I wandered back through the park the daydreams started up again. I was already putting my outfit together for the date of the century and fast-forwarding to the kiss.

What would it be like? God I felt sick with excitement. This really was one of the opportunities Janis Joplin was telling me about through her music – as far as John was concerned, I really needed to get him while I could.

I dropped Trevor off back home, unhooked his lead, opened the kitchen door so he could get to his water and rice, and quickly did a U-turn to head into work.

It's amazing how much a little potential romance can knock your concentration. And it's also amazing how much chaos a misplaced decimal point can cause. One tiny little mistake and all that chaos.

I spent about 45 minutes trying to reverse the order I had just faxed through for 1500 caravan bathrooms and replace it with a rather more sensible order of 15 caravan bathrooms.

And then I realised I had shredded the contents of my in-tray rather than my to-shred-tray, so was left with literally no idea what I was meant to be doing or what I needed to somehow hunt down a photocopy of.

But it wasn't enough to stop me smiling inside. Dreaming of the wedding. Dave in a bridesmaid's dress. Claire remaining fully clothed...Dad giving a speech about my climbing frame mishap...

However, just when the office was filling up with coffee-break chatter, I idly wandered over to the communal fridge to grab my lunch. I was still daydreaming of bridesmaids...speeches...and cake.

I opened the fridge, wrinkling my nose as I wondered whose lunch was well past its sell by date, grabbed my lunchbox, filled a glass of water from the cooler and wandered back to my desk. Shane and the sycophant had strolled over already and were telling another mythical story about Shane's pulling prowess.

Tossers.

And then I opened my lunchbox.

That was not a ham and cucumber sandwich staring back at me. Instead of my tasty sarnie, I had pulled the plastic top off and exposed the entire office to a pile of stinking doggie poop in a sandwich bag.

I'd forgotten to replenish my packed lunch that morning in the hurry! Well, I'd replenished it, but not with a wholesome lunch. I'd left it in my work bag as I dashed out the house in haste this morning. Poor retro Snoopy lunch box had spent the day hosting a festering pile of poop. I was supposed to pick up the light blue lunchbox with a bird pattern all over it.

Shane roared with laughter. The sycophant was sick. And Mike thinks there's something very, very wrong with me.

'Emma. Could I have a word please?'

Oh God. I've really done it now. I'm going to be sacked.

CHAPTER 6

The thoughts racing through my brain were beyond worrying. Signing on at the job centre. Queuing up to answer questions like a guilty shirker. I'd been there before. I did not want to go back.

I just couldn't face the thought of it. It was time to grovel.

'Look. Mike. I'm so sorry. I know I've been late. I know I messed that order up. But…'

'Yep. Your admin skills aren't the best really, are they?'

Here we go…

'Which is why I've been thinking of offering you a promotion.'

What the fuck?

'Sorry, what?'

'Yes. I think you'd be a great asset to the sales team. And with one of the team heading back to uni in September, I've decided to have a mini restructure. And I thought of you. You need a challenge, Emma. And admin just isn't doing it for you. You're talented Emma. You need something that better utilises your communications skills.'

Sales? Oh God. That means working with Shane and the sycophant.

'You'd be reporting directly into Dave.'

Maybe it wouldn't be so bad after all.

'What would I be doing?'

Mike explained the role to me. It was a sales role but with more of a marketing bent. It was about using my written skills to create sales material, and using my analytical skills to target the communications effectively. Mike knew how proud I was of my degree, and he reckoned this was a chance to use some of my creativity.

He printed out a job description and told me to go home and have a think about it. There was a pretty decent pay rise involved too.

'I really think you could go places, Emma. You could have a bright future here. I could see you progressing to the top one day.'

It felt amazing to see that somebody really believed in me. But could I really get passionate about selling caravans? They didn't especially figure in my dream holiday, but maybe I needed to think about it from a different point of view? We all enjoy different things don't we. Some people like rocking out to Nirvana at Spiders, some people like bopping to Shaggy at LAs. I just had to consider who I was writing for and remember it wasn't all about me, me, me.

Saying that, my skills and passion would certainly be far better suited to working in a record shop. I could easily write lines about the new sounds from The Breeders or the old sounds from Nirvana. I could definitely get excited about that.

But that was too close to the 27 club. Not only would I be enjoying rock music, I'd be living it. Personally and professionally. Just like the members of the 27 club were. You really have to be careful what you wish for.

As they say, though, stress isn't just about being too busy - it's also about being too bored. And aside from Claire's hilarious tales in the office, the job completely and utterly bored me. I wasn't using my brain in its natural and preferred capacity.

I headed home with the job description, studying it closely while sitting on the top deck of the crowded, bumpy bus. It sounded quite interesting, and it could be a refreshing change. I'd be creating sales material, not just filing it away. I'd be able to leave my stamp on something. Play a part. Have a say.

It made me re-evaluate what I was good at.

Admin involves organising and managing time and activities well. I was not the most organised of people. My desk always looked like a bomb had hit it and Mike always commented on my 'organised chaos' – which was kind of him really, given it was purely just chaos. There was no structure to it.

But this job involved writing creatively about caravans to encourage people to buy them. I was definitely better at thinking creatively. I enjoyed thinking creatively. My mind was very good at wandering off on its own tangents. Maybe I *would* be good at this? Maybe I could make a real difference to our sales targets and our image?

I started to wonder what it was that made us good at some things and not others. Was it a skill we learned? Was it a part of our personality? Was it experience? There was definitely that whole left-brain, right-brain argument.

If you're left-brained, you're analytical and methodical. Basically, you need to be left-brained to be good at admin and finance and science and stuff.

If you're right-brained, you're creative.

In some ways, I could see I fitted in both camps. I loved the analytical side to my Criminology degree. But I think it was the leaps in thinking and the curiosity that really drove me. As well as finding creative ways to tackle a problem.

I very certainly had some right-brain traits. That's what Mike seemed to be saying. And that's what the job description was asking for - a creative approach to writing sales adverts and literature. Identifying selling points in new static home designs. Conjuring up the experience of a caravanning holiday. That's all right-brained stuff.

And of course, playing the guitar, loving music - good music - that's all right-brained too.

The 27 club members were certainly all right-brained. They couldn't have achieved what they did without flexing their artistic muscles.

Jim Morrison was a poet. A rider on the storm. A lizard king.

Kurt Cobain was known to be a brilliantly dark artist as well as a beautiful songwriter.

And Jimi Hendrix...well...playing the guitar like that certainly can't be down to science. Jimi Hendrix could play the guitar with his teeth for God's sake. In fact, there was a rumour he could play the guitar without touching the guitar at all!

From what I'd read, Jimi Hendrix didn't have the best childhood. Like my mum, his mother was really quite young when she had him. And his upbringing was precarious, with his parents struggling with money and alcohol. You have to wonder whether it was the trauma of his childhood that led to a barbiturates overdose, or whether it was the trauma of being a famous rock star?

Or what if the successful, right-brained members of the population are doomed to early expiration? What if using your brain in that way wears it out quicker? What if there's a correlation between being left-handed and right-brained and early death.

I am left-handed and right-brained. Just like Jimi Hendrix. That surely must place a lot of pressure on the old noggin. I mean, how many people can flip a right-handed guitar upside down and play it backwards, and then become known as one of the best guitarists of our time?

Being pulled in two different directions was no good for anyone. I needed to streamline. Maybe I needed to practice being more left-brained. Or more right-handed?

The pull in opposite directions could be the reason why I'm so clumsy.

So many what-ifs.

I folded up the job description and put it in my bag and looked up to the front of the bus. We were just heading around the corner when I noticed the bus felt more wobbly than usual. As we veered towards the left, something didn't feel right. The horizon became unstable and my heart started pounding.

I was feeling faint again. What the hell was up with my blood pressure? I held onto the rail in front of me and with my other hand, took the job description back out of my bag to take my mind off things. But the words on the page were blurred, just like the horizon. My hands started to feel tingly again and, without thinking, I pinged the bell alerting the driver to stop, and made my way quickly down the stairs, dropping the Shaw's Static Holiday Homes headed paper as I left my seat.

Everything felt wobbly and unreal. I could almost imagine the bus toppling over and a sense of dread overpowered me. Finally, just as my breathing was starting to speed up, the bus pulled into the stop and opened its doors. I hopped off the wobbly container and onto the pavement, feeling relieved to feel the ground beneath my feet and the fresh air in my nostrils.

I was a few stops from home but the walk did me good. My hands no longer tingled and the horizon was sharply in focus. I reminded myself that I needed to see the doctor about this. Maybe I needed to eat more red meat or something?

Career changes. Dietary changes. Crikey, it was all happening at once.

Speaking of big events, it was the night that Question Time was coming to Hull. And it turned out Dad and Bob could really pull a crowd.

I'll give it its due, the poster must have really appealed to the Angel crowd. But even though I could see the appeal in watching them on TV – I certainly wouldn't have dared go live on BBC Question Time myself. Pretty brave when you think about it. I can't imagine any of the other punters would do it either. It just wasn't something folk round here got the chance to do.

The excitement in the bar was palpable. It was like we were at a televised World Cup game.

Honestly, I know people queue outside gigs five hours in advance, but at this rate, the entire pub was going to be on the bleedin' floor in a pool of vomit by the time Dad and Bob made it in front of the cameras. We still had two hours to go and they were all getting in extra pints and whiskey chasers so as to avoid queuing at the bar mid-question and missing Dad and Bob.

I decided to order a lime and soda. I needed to take it steady this evening after my recent wobbles.

Dave had offered to help Brenda behind the bar to make up for Bob's absence. He was promised free beer, so that sweetened the deal. And the big screen was placed so that everyone working and drinking could see it (there was a major crossover there so that was easy).

I don't imagine there's ever been such a round of applause and whooping for BBC Question Time before, but The Angel was on its feet when the theme tune began.

As David Dimbleby walked towards the camera, introducing his guests and stating their location (big up Hull University) there he was. In the background. Best shirt and tie on. Looking directly at the camera while also awkwardly fidgeting in his seat. My politically astute father. About to have his moment. About to make an impact for the greater good.

'Go on son!'

Dear. God. It was one of the old guys in the raincoats. I didn't know they spoke. I'm not sure which one it was, though. Unless they spoke in unison.

My dad's appearance, however, on closer inspection, looked ever so slightly intoxicated. How the hell did he manage that? How the hell did he get into the studio in that state?

'Hang on, where's my Bob?' Brenda shouted out.

Good point. Where was Bob? Sitting next to my Dad was an empty seat. But then, all of a sudden, Bob's head appeared from nowhere. He must have been tying his shoelaces or something.

'Ah there's me fella.' Brenda piped up again sounding much happier now.

But then Dad disappeared from view, and Bob was seemingly sitting next to an empty seat.

'What are they doing?' I asked nobody in particular. Then it occurred to me. Bob had his bloody hip flask down there!

Dad popped up again just as the camera moved in on him for his question. That was a close call. He'd nearly missed his moment.

'I'd like to ask Edwina...'

Oh good God. I could barely look. What was he thinking? He was supposed to be there for Hull. For socialism. For the people. Not questioning Edwina about her apparently fictitious sex-romp novel.

John Prescott had a smirk on his face. Dimbleby looked slightly shaken. But when Edwina didn't flinch, Dad and Bob sprung into action.

'We stand for Hull's dairy farmers.' Booming out from a now fully standing Bob, who appeared to have...what was that...an egg in his hand?

Said egg was catapulted through the air.

Dear God.

'Go on son!'

Hull's finest free-range produce went hurtling through the live studio air.

The look on Edwina's face, however, never changed.

The egg hit John Prescott. Man of the people. Man of Hull. Man of the Labour Party.

As the yellow shiny gloop slid off his greying hair and onto his suit jacket, the smirk changed into something less amenable. The anger. My God, the anger...his face turned purple. Like a piece of uncooked bacon.

That'd certainly give you food poisoning even if the eggs didn't.

But why could an egg really make so many people so angry? Especially Mr Prescott. After all, didn't Labour advocate for the safety of eggs? There was no salmonella on his shirt. Just the ingredients for a nice omelette.

The camera turned back to Dimbleby, who was blatantly getting the voice of a panicked TV producer in his ear. Meanwhile, the audience continued to be disrupted as two wobbly middle-aged Hull blokes frantically made for the exit, security in tow.

The pub was silent. Eyes fixated on the big screen. Pints frozen in mid-air.

Surely John Prescott would understand? He was a Hull bloke, just like these two wallies.

The atmosphere in The Angel deflated like a whoopie cushion. Quickly and uncomfortably. The pitch had changed. It was like one great big slow shake of the head. A low rumble of disappointing thunder. An audible tut.

Dad and Bob went on national TV to tackle the Tories. And instead they spattered John Prescott with an egg. I hoped to God it didn't contain salmonella. Imagine the Hull Daily Mail headlines.

'Drinks are on the house folks. Least we can do.' Shouted Brenda, shaking her head as she walked past her wedding picture on the shelf behind the bar.

Doreen lifted her empty glass with a nod and a smirk. Her eyes were practically shut at this point. She must've been in here since opening.

I felt a lock-in coming on. Dad and Bob had let the people down so sorrows must be drowned. They'd catapulted one of their own.

Dave, on the other hand, found it all hilarious, and the overall tone reverted slightly as quadruple Drambuie's were being downed as quickly as they were being poured. Anarchy in the Angel. This was not the desired effect.

Still, if you can't beat them.

I had told myself to go steady that night. I'd had too many hangovers of late and they all led to bad places. And I still didn't know why I kept feeling faint. But I couldn't face the aftermath of Question Time without a little bevvy or two. The thing was, in addition to the wobbles, cystitis had made a very unwelcome return to my nether regions. I used to get it all the time as a kid, and it had been threatening on and off for the last few days. Hence, I was in and out of the loos like a yo-yo and the alcohol really wasn't helping matters. God knows how I managed to sit through the whole of Question Time.

'What the hell's up with you? You're pissing like a racehorse. Or have you caught IB-wotsit off Trevor?' Dave was quizzing me.

'You can't catch IBS, Dave. It's not contagious. I've just got cystitis. All women get it. Makes us run to the loo urgently every two minutes. It's no biggie.'

He nodded. Looking slightly confused and taken aback.

'Karaoke, Emma?'

The next morning, I didn't wake up feeling the joys of Spring at all. The sun was once more shining, but I was about to head into work with the mother of all hangovers.

I made a mental note of forgiveness telling myself that nobody could see their Dad's first appearance on live prime time telly sober.

Anyway, at least I was doing well with Trev's diet. He was enjoying fresh chicken breast for breakfast and tea, with a few little doggy treats thrown in for good measure. The vet did indeed confirm it was a case of doggy IBS that my boy (and my carpet) was suffering from, so chicken and rice was the meal du jour from now on.

So I guess the poopy lunch box incident was worth it – I'd obviously managed to scoop enough to get the diagnosis.

After feeding Trev his gourmet breakfast, I brushed the fine sugary coating of Drambuie from my teeth, swept my hair into a quick ponytail and headed out the door with a slice of buttery toast hanging from my mouth as I locked up.

I decided to sit on the lower deck of the bus this time.

As I arrived at work, it seemed that news of my potential promotion had spread. And Shane and the sycophant made it very clear they were not impressed.

'You've no sales experience. One minute your faxing orders, the next you're tipped to be the next big thing in sales. Fuck's sake.'

I hadn't even said yes, yet. And it was already getting them wound up. To be honest, I thought, that's probably just given me a rock-solid reason to accept the promotion.

I'd be the only female in sales. I'd be infiltrating their male bravado bollocks. I'd be able to shut down the sexist club chat about the fake fingering of female colleagues on the dance floor.

Banter they say. Yeah, right. And I'd only heard the gossip they brought into the main office. God knows what it's like when they're left to their own devices.

Shane's snide comment made me think about that poor guitarist though. The one who couldn't play a note one day and had the talent of Eric Clapton the next.

And then, of course, dead the next.

Were they right? I didn't have any experience, so how could Mike think I'd be any good at it? What was he going on? It's not as if he'd ever read my dissertation. Was my promotion the biggest blag in the history of caravan sales?

Maybe finding yourself an imposter in somebody else's world is the very thing that drives rock stars to drugs or suicide. I mean, look at Sid Vicious. He couldn't play. And he was even younger when he died of an overdose.

Oh God, maybe the ones who achieve success without the experience or substance to back it up die even sooner. At the very least, I felt in danger of fucking this new job right up.

It was sales too. I felt slightly uncomfortable about it. Like it was the corporate, capitalist world Dad was always banging on about. Profit driven sales environments. He says that's what creates hell. He says it's led by rich capitalist selfish sinners. I would be an imposter in an unfriendly world.

Or perhaps I was just trying to talk myself out of it. Maybe I was just nervous?

I couldn't answer straight away. Mike was giving me a while to think about it anyway, given the other guy wasn't leaving until September. So there was time to mull it over.

Maybe chasing success in the run up to your 27th birthday wasn't the wisest thing to do. Perhaps change was the last thing I needed at that point.

Regardless, Claire decided we needed to head out of the office and have a '*proper dinner, somewhere nice*' to celebrate the job offer. I still wasn't sure there was anything to celebrate but a lunch away from the office was always a good thing, rare as it was.

She drove us away from the industrial site, and towards the avenues where we could get something decent to eat. '*Nouveau cuisine*' she said. Although that's not actually what we were after or indeed about to get.

The businesses on the estate were generally well catered for when it came to lunch times, but health-focussed foodies were not. It was all burger vans parked up outside businesses where the usual order was hamburger with fried onions, a can of tango, and a packet of salt 'n' vinegar.

That was the usual order because there was little else to spice your lunch time up with – aside from brown sauce.

Claire had heard of a nice little vegetarian place which she said we should try to 'broaden our repertoire'. After all, it was my celebration not hers and she knew I was trying to live a purer lifestyle.

As we arrived, I noticed it was one of those places that looks way cooler and way posher than the others purely because it's so simple. It wasn't trying too hard. Or maybe it was? The menu was chalked up on a board, and the rickety chairs and tables looked right at home on the wobbly stone floor. None of them seemed to match. Were they all left there in the building when the café owners bought it, or did they meticulously hunt down specific chairs and tables over several years to achieve this bric-a-brac effect? Whatever, it worked for me. I liked it.

'Nice in here, innit?' Claire said as we walked in, but I knew it wasn't really her cup of tea, from the way she looked the place up and down. Her father was Hull's most successful burger bar owner. I don't imagine tofu had ever passed her lips.

Before we even got to the food, we realised that they literally didn't seem to do Claire's cup of tea. It was all red bush and peppermint. English breakfast, it seemed, was not on the menu. At least, it wasn't something they shouted about anyway.

I was grateful to her thoughtfulness though and I was looking forward to a smoky lentil chilli with a ton of cheese on top because, well, I was celebrating a new job offer. And it certainly made a change from my plain cheese and ham sarnies.

In fact, since the Snoopy lunch box incident I'd been bringing my sandwiches pre-packed from Boots on my way in to work. I couldn't risk another poo-based incident.

So it was lovely having Claire go out of her way for me today. Really sweet in fact.

We took a seat and she ordered potato wedges and a glass of orange juice. Said she was a little suspicious of vegetarian food that was dressed up in traditionally meat-dish flavours. I went all in for the chilli and ordered a 'real lemonade' to go with it.

After a few cursory comments about the promotion and how I'd be able to shake up the lads, the conversation managed to get swamped by talk of her weekend sexploits and subsequent telephone exchanges. Honestly, I think I'd rather watch *9 lives of a wet pussy* nine times over than listen to some of this sordid detail.

'You should be charging for this material, Claire. You'd make a fortune.'

'Yeah, I know. Just last week, Pete gave me a twenty and winked before he went home. So sweet. Lovely bloke, him.'

I think she was missing the insinuation. For all the rough and explicit chatter, she was deeply innocent at heart. Well,

OK, deeply naïve maybe. She wondered why she never heard from him again.

'How you getting on with John the dog walker, anyway?'

'Yeah, he's definitely got potential.' I said, my thoughts moving away from Claire and back into my daydreams.

We continued lunch, pondering over John the dog walker, Shane and the sycophant's response to my promotion and whether, if we had to pick one or face certain death by torture, would we rather shag 80s mulleted popstars Glenn Madeiros or Owen Paul?

We paid the bill and were just gathering up our things from under our chairs when Claire suddenly stopped.

'Ooh. Before I go. I've got you a well-done gift.'

It was wrapped, but it certainly didn't look like a book on succeeding in business. Or indeed a box of chocolates.

'Something to get you started. Oh! Ha ha! Geddit!'

And with that, in the busy wholesome vegetarian cafe, I opened the lovingly wrapped package containing….

'What is it?' I asked, looking carefully at the pink tower with beads in the middle. At first I thought it might be some kind of sweetie toy machine. You know, like gumballs or something. Until I realised the, um, recognisable helmet shape at the top.

'This' said Claire loudly and proudly. 'Is the Jack Rabbit vibrator.'

What on earth was Claire doing buying me a vibrator?

'Um. Thanks.' I very quickly hid it on my lap under the table, realising that hiding it 'down below' might be even worse than having it out on show.

'Me auntie held one of those parties, you know, with all the sex toys and that. They had a special deal, two for one, I thought, well this'll be a good way for Emma to celebrate that job offer!'

I was speechless.

'I didn't think you'd want anything too crass. Hence the colour.'

Unfortunately, the fact that it was a cute lilac colour didn't really stop the other customers in the cafe from looking embarrassed, giggly or disgusted in equal measures. And it was certainly of generous proportions.

Was that a compliment, or an insult?

I'd never seen anything like it. I mean, sure, I'd seen a vibrator, but nothing with rabbit ears positioned halfway down it. Mind, given that John still hadn't called me, maybe this was just what I needed. I was fast losing hope on the romance front.

'I'm telling you now. These things are going to be big, baby.' Claire added with a twinkle in her eye.

Ugh. So now I know she's tried and tested one. I did not want those images swirling around my head just after eating.

At this point I was regretting the careless nature of my unwrapping given it was going to be pretty difficult to cover Claire's thoughtful gift back up with the little scraps of wrapping paper I had let fall to the floor like confetti. Shit.

'Right then, let's get back to work.'

And with that we were off. And I had nothing to wrap or carry my lovely congratulatory gift in. There was no way that monster rabbit was going to fit into my little canvas bag. So I walked out as quickly and awkwardly as I possibly could, while wishing Claire would slow down on the busy shopping street so I could ask her to pop it back in her bag where it came from.

Must buy a bigger work bag.

The embarrassment took me right back to my high school days. The days before I discovered non-applicator tampons thanks to all that Lil-lets advertising in *Just 17* magazine. The days of needing to change said tampon and having to sneak past Adam Haydock and Stuart Taylforth to leave Geography class with a giant Tampax in my hand. It was that. Or a bloody leakage.

Stay calm, Emma. They are not here.

But my dad was.

'Hey, Emma. What's this you've got then?'

For fuck's sake. Could he have timed this any better? I guess it was a fair swap – I had to endure the knowledge that he was watching porn on my Apollo video account, and he had to endure the knowledge that…well, would he even know if I lied about what it was.

'Hi, Dad. It's a new toy for Trev. Anyway, can't stop. Late back from lunchbreak.'

We headed back to the office with the Jack Rabbit stuffed up my coat sleeve for safety. I smuggled it through the office and hid it in my desk drawer. I mean, I was hardly going to stand it up in all its glory next to the plastic plant pot was I?

After the huge veggie chilli 'n' cheese lunch I was starting to feel sleepy and it was hard work trying to stop myself yawning all afternoon. I grabbed a second Diet Coke and knocked it back, giving myself a ten-minute buzz before feeling even worse than I did before I had it.

It seemed to be a truth that anything we try to rush tends to have a negative effect. We try to wake ourselves up with a big dose of caffeine – and end up feeling even more sleepy. We try to catch up with the other drinkers by necking a shot, and we end up racing straight past them to the pass-out finish line. But I was contemplating rushing into a promotion in an area I had no previous experience in, and Claire was suggesting we all orgasm in a hurry with exciting new sex toy technology.

Everyone was in a rush these days. A rush to live life to the fullest and experience it all before we actually grew up. And a rush to die aged 27.

Get it while you can.

I left the office at 5.30pm on the dot in a rush to get home. No – not to try out the Jack Rabbit. In fact, I was just desperate to get out of the office, get some fresh air and wake myself up. Having the responsibility of a dog can really come in handy when you need to practice a little self-care but seemingly don't care enough about yourself to do so.

I loved having Trev for company but I was starting to wonder what it might be like to have an actual human partner in crime living in the same house as me. Much as I loved Dad and Dave, I couldn't live with either of them. Not full time, anyway. But there was something lovely about the idea of opening the front door and shouting *'you'll never guess what Claire bought me today'* whilst taking off my shoes and dropping my keys in the pot.

Trev wouldn't really get the joke. He'd probably try to bury it in the garden. That'd make for an amusing time capsule for our future school children.

I'd always enjoyed my independence – which probably came from being an only child and Mum leaving us when I was so young. But there's something to be said for playing along with Blockbusters and having somebody witness you getting the answers right.

I'll have a 'p' please Bob.

What 'p' will make you a cup of tea, rub your feet and congratulate you for getting this question right.

A partner, Bob.

Whilst I was missing the human interactions of an evening, at work, I seemed to be getting a huge amount of Claire's attention. And pity so it seemed. She appeared to be gravely concerned about me. And I couldn't understand why.

She brought me over a cuppa (never happens) and handed it to me with a look of pity on her face as she perched on my desk, cupping her own warm cup of tea tight in her hands.

'Oh Emma.'

'What?' I asked, waiting for a joke or something to come hurtling towards me.

'Look, Emma.' She was touching my hand across the desk looking really serious. This was really weird. 'I know it's hard to talk about it. I know it's, you know, a bit embarrassing. But I reckon you need to just get it all out,

OK lovely? How are you feeling?'

What was she talking about?

'What are you talking about?'

'Aw sweetheart, you don't need to pretend with me. We tell each other everything. There's nothing to be ashamed of.'

'Is this about the promotion gossip? I'm not bothered by them, you know. I don't even know if I'm taking it yet.'

'No, course it's not about that Emma. I'm chuffed to bits for you. Although I really hope you can keep this desk. Can't miss my gossip buddy. No, it's about *the other thing*.' She mouthed those final three words as if a curse might be placed upon her if she spoke them out loud.

I was still confused.

'I'm guessing this is the reason you were toying with celibacy?' She asked.

'Sorry, what?'

'I've heard it can make you lose your mind. Bring you out in sores and all sorts. I've read about it. You must see your doctor. Before it attacks your brain cells Emma. Honestly. I don't want to panic you. But I'm really worried about you.'

'Working in sales? Yep that can certainly make you lose your mind. But sores? What on earth are you talking about' I was half ignoring the chat and half baffled. But Claire was often gibbering on about something or nothing so I carried on stapling the order forms to the invoices.

'You must take this seriously Emma. I couldn't believe it when I heard. But what with Pete from the cabby shop drinking in The Angel an' everything. But then he told Shane which I think was some kind of sabotage plan cos the lads are all jealous of your promotion.'

'I haven't even been promoted yet Claire!'

She carried on.

'So of course, we all know now. Oh but, I mean, don't worry about that. They're all just a bunch of knobheads, Emma. I told 'em where to stick it when they were taking the piss. Bloody kids. Just ignore them.'

'Claire, seriously. What are you talking about?'

'You know. Your problems *down below*.' Again, the last two words were mouthed as if she daren't speak them. Very strange for someone like Claire to become coy all of a sudden. Weirdly though, I couldn't remember telling her about the cystitis. Must've done at some point, I guessed.

'Oh that! Yeah it's a right pain having your waters infected. I've been bleeding a little this time too. Honestly, the agony. I get it all the time though. What can you do.'

'Well, for starters you can be more careful. It only takes the one time, Emma. You know that.'

One time of what?

She walked over to her desk and began rifling through her secret biscuit stash in the filing drawer, which she then closed with a sigh. She'd given up on the search for a jammy dodger. She turned to me, resigned.

'Look. It obviously hasn't progressed too far. I mean, there's no visible rash or anything.'

'Rash?'

'You're in denial. I get that. Was it someone you don't want to see again who infected you?'

'You don't need to have sex to get it, Claire. Just having too much to drink can knock you off kilter.'

'Well, yes. Getting blind drunk can make you do stupid things. Make stupid decisions. Forget to use a condom. Here, I picked up a leaflet in the clinic for you.'

'I don't need a leaflet. I just need a glass of cranberry juice.'

She produced said leaflet from her handbag.

Syphilis. Symptoms, facts and treatment options.

What the fuck.

'What the fuck's this got to do with me?'

'Dave said...'

Fuck's sake, Dave!

CHAPTER 7

'You say tomato…'

'There's a bit of a difference between cystitis and syphilis, Dave. It's not just how you pronounce them.'

'But you told me you had...'

'Cystitis! I have cystitis!'

'Sorry, Emma. I got it wrong, OK.'

I tried to imagine the number of people who, at this moment in time, believed I had syphilis. I winced at the thought of the cat calls. The names. *Syphilitic Emma. V D Barclay.* I mean, who gets words like that confused?

Claire mentioned they'd been taking bets in the factory on who the prime suspect was. Who'd given me the poisonous dose. Apparently the sycophant was in the running. Jesus Christ – did they really think that badly of me?

I tried to shake the thoughts away. Who cared anyway? It wasn't as though I'd always had dreams of climbing the ranks of a caravan firm. I wanted to be a criminologist. I wasn't even sure I wanted that promotion. I might get a new job and never have to see them again.

Dave wasn't his usual self at all that day when he'd called over for a quick cuppa. He was far too quick to apologise. And he hadn't had any fun with the STD confusion. I thought he'd be creasing about that and giving me even more grief. But he wasn't. He was pretty quiet, actually.

The last time he sounded like this was after England's defeat against Germany in Italia 90. Or was it? When I think about it, he didn't sound so great on the answerphone message he left me this morning.

Something was amiss. I could tell.

'What's up, Dave?'

'Ah. Nothing really. I'm fine.'

'Oh right. Got a lot of work on at the minute?'

'Yeah, it's going OK.'

This was awkward. Our conversation was never awkward.

I tried to get the banter going. 'Did I tell you about the Jack Rabbit vibrator bloody Claire got me. Honestly, Dave, I've never been so mortified. She got it out in the middle of…'

'She's a cracker that one.'

'Is that all you're going to say? Did you not hear me? Claire presented me with a purple vibrator with rabbit ears right in the middle of..'

'..I heard!' Dave snapped at me. He never snapped at me.

'Dave, what's up?'

'Nowt. I told you. Anyway, I've got to get off.'

He stood up to leave, but I wasn't having any of it. This was not the Dave I knew.

'Sit back down!' I ordered. He looked resigned and defeated. He sat back in his seat, rolling his eyes.

'You better tell me what's going on Dave Chapman or I'm not letting you out this house.'

'I've just been a bit under the weather, that's all.'

'How so?' I asked.

'Just, you know, a bit achy and stuff. I thought it was the flu.'

'Bloody man flu.' I joked, instantly regretting it when I saw the look he shot me. 'Shit, sorry mate. Seriously, are you OK?'

'Well, the aches and pains never did turn into anything fluey. And when I thought about it, they were concentrated mainly in one place.' He said, whilst kind of nodding to his nether regions. 'I thought I must have knackered my knackers playing footie or something. I mean, I've never been good at…'

'Dave. Tell me straight. What is it.'

'I've got ball cancer, Emma.'

I felt like someone had hit me over the head with a mallet. What did he just say?

'What did you just say?'

'Ball cancer.'

I was horrified. Cancer. The c-word. The big, bad c-word.

'Cancer?'

It was the one word I didn't want to think about at this very moment in time and yet I couldn't stop myself saying it.

'Ball cancer?'

Once the sledgehammer settled in the pit of my stomach, he explained it all to me.

He'd had some pain. Sitting down quickly was the main culprit. But he didn't think too much of it. He'd just played a charity football match for work so maybe he'd hurt it then. A kick in the balls with the bottom of a football boot was not to be sniffed at. But he couldn't remember it happening.

It was playing on his mind so he had a feel around and there it was. A lump. He said he was pretty calm at first. Men do get lumps down there after all. It was probably nothing. But he went to the GP surgery anyway.

He was hoping his doctor would simply put his mind at rest, but he said he knew the minute the doctor felt it. Just from the look on her face. This was serious.

They got him in for a scan as a matter of urgency. It was probably nothing, they said. It could be a cyst or a benign tumour. But just to be safe, he should go for a scan.

Turns out, the word benign didn't feature in his diagnosis at all. This was the real deal. This was the big C.

My heart was pounding. My hands tingling. I wanted to cry. But I needed to be strong.

He said he was going to be OK. They were getting him in ASAP for surgery. Apparently, he'd caught it early.

I was distraught. He was too young for any of this shit, surely? And why has he been through all this – appointments, scans, without telling me. Why did he keep it all to himself? He could have talked to me. I almost felt angry with him.

He stood up to leave but I made him promise to come over for his tea that week. My heart aching and racing in equal measures. I'd just had a massive go at him over his silly little word mix-up and all along, his nether regions were dealing with something far worse than mine were reputed to be getting kicked by.

My eyes were tight shut but all I could see was Dave. Dead. Cold. His funeral. Oasis playing in The Angel for the wake. Everyone blubbing as they chanted the lyrics to *'Live Forever'.* Bob putting out the vol au vents and Brenda cracking open the single malt. Why was I always thinking about death?

I cursed myself for being so negative. But Dave had already turned 27. It seemed the myth was coming true in the cruellest of ways.

We both loved rock 'n' roll. We both had a little too much fun with cigarettes and alcohol. We never went to church. We didn't live a wholesome life.

What the fuck is it about twenty-bleedin'-seven.

Was there any way to get Dave off this terrifying rollercoaster? Did Kurt or Janis or Jim ever have this opportunity. To see what might lie ahead and rectify it? We had a chance here. A real chance. And I had to help him. He needed me. And my God, I needed him.

I decided to do the only thing I could to demonstrate my true feelings for my best mate. I set about making him a compilation tape. I needed him to know how I felt, and as much as we could tell each other anything, this felt like the best way of doing it. Of getting the emotions out there.

It was a serious business making a compilation tape – especially one for someone you cared about. And I needed it to be perfect. This was the biggest and most important reason I had ever had to compile the perfect track list. I sat down in front of my hi-fi and found a blank tape. I tried to discipline my thoughts. They were racing off with catastrophes about his treatment making him ill, or not working, or something out of the blue happening and him not even making it for his tea. I needed to focus my mind. I needed something to concentrate on. Perhaps the compilation tape was as much for me as it was for him. I took a deep breath and focused on the task in hand.

I was something of a master at mix-tape creation.

The key things to consider in the making of a compilation tape are:

1. Have you got a clean, unused tape?

If not, you must immediately head to Wilkos or Woolworths and buy a new one. The artistic wording and dedication to the intended recipient of said tape must be a priority. They must know that this whole project was designed especially for them. The tape would simply not work for another human being.

2. How long should the tape be?

Do you go for the 45, the 60 or the 90-minute tape? If it's too short, you'll never be able to say everything you need to say. If it's too long, you'll dilute its impact with tenuous, half-decent tracks from the charts that mean nothing. I opted for the 60-minute TDK.

3. What are you trying to say?

What's the key message of the compilation tape? For a new boyfriend/girlfriend you're most likely going to be showing off your musical knowledge and diversity by including the stuff they may not have heard before. But at the same time, it needs to evoke feelings of love and romance in an edgy and appealing way. It needs to show your hidden depths. In this instance, the proposed tape was for my best mate who had just found out he had testicular cancer. And I'd just had a massive go at him for telling people I had syphilis instead of cystitis. So, it needed, first of all, to say sorry. Secondly, it needed to remind him that we were best mates and that he meant the world to me. Thirdly, it needed to recognise what he was going through – the pain, the fear. Lastly, it needed to instil hope. Ooh this was a tough one. This was a rollercoaster ride far more intricate than anything Alton Towers might come up with.

4. What formats are you recording from?

Once you've chosen your tracks, you needed to audit the various formats you were recording from. CD to tape – creates a perfect sound. Bought tape to tape, again, high quality. Recorded tape to recorded tape, well, that could be a bit meh – mainly because the source format could be compromised. Record to tape, well this was usually quieter still, and often had a crackle (but you could argue that it's atmospheric). Finally, and this is one that you should only ever use if you absolutely have to, recording from Sunday night's top 40 countdown on Radio 1 was, frankly, a high risk strategy. This should only be attempted by those with exceptional reaction times. The finger needs to be hovering over the pause button on high alert, ready to estimate the exact time when the voice of Bruno Brookes will come barging into your perfect audio love letter. Thankfully, there was nothing in the charts that I wanted to include on this one, and frankly, no time to wait for the official charts to be announced.

5. The order

Just like a Pink Floyd album, the compilation tape has to be a high-concept album with messages more powerful than a Bonnie Tyler ballad (I could just about get away with Bonnie Tyler – my dad used to play it in the car). And to be effective at this, you need to carefully consider the order of the tracks. Do you want to finish on a high? Do you want to finish on an invitation for sex? Or do you want to make your now ex-boyfriend feel thoroughly regretful of their decision to dump you last week when they just snogged Becky Thompson in the pub car park having been relentlessly allured by the scent of her new Exclamation perfume. The album must make sense. It must tell a story to fulfil its purpose.

6. The album sleeve

You can be quite creative with a biro and a piece of lined card when you put your mind to it. The font is key – is it strictly neat and legible? Or is it an artistic approach reminiscent of a horror movie title or a fairy tale book cover? Icons are your friend here too. Throwing a star or a heart between the artist and the song is a great way to express yourself whilst differentiating between the two (very important when you have songs such as S:Express by S:Express). And finally, you won't go wrong with a multi-coloured biro pen. Use the colour to denote the mood. Genius.

I placed all of my CDs, records and tapes over the floor and set about building my audio story. Sorry, Dave's audio story. His journey. His emotional rollercoaster that was going to leave him floating on a natural happy high. The final collection became a contemplative side A, with an upbeat side B:

Side A
1. Mad World by Tears for Fears
2. Where is my Mind? by The Pixies
3. Riders on the Storm by The Doors
4. Live Through This by Hole

5. Bridge over Troubled Water by Simon and Garfunkel

Side B

1. Movin' on Up by Primal Scream
2. Best Friend by The Senseless Things
3. You and Me Song by The Wannadies
4. Rise and Shine by The Cardigans
5. Live Forever by Oasis

I was happy with this rushed work of art. I rewound the tape, placed it in its box and carefully wrote the titles on the sleeve.

When my dinner date with Dave came around, I hit the kitchen. I could have made a chicken cacciatore. Or a chicken and mushroom risotto. But I knew better than anyone what Dave would appreciate for his tea. I turned the oven to the standard 180 degrees (the temperature at which everything seems to cook to perfection in a fan oven) then put my feet up with a cuppa.

When the doorbell rang even Trev seemed to be barking considerately, applying a lower-than-usual-volume to his alarm call. I went to the door and could see the outline of Dave. Big, strong Dave in his parka. He had his fluffy head down (his brown hair was finally starting to return to its former glory), but that was his usual stance.

I opened the door and gave him and his damp rainy coat a big bear hug. He breathed in the aromas emanating from my kitchen:

'Mmm Findus crispy pancakes. Emma you beaut.'

He headed straight towards the kitchen to confirm his suspicions about tea and grab himself a Coke from the fridge.

'Ahhhh' He smacked his lips and shot me a wink.

'Listen, Dave, we need to talk.'

'If we must.'

He sighed a big sigh, plonked himself in the armchair and tapped the seat for Trev to jump up.

'How you doing?' I asked. Stupid question, on reflection.

'I'm doing fine, Emma. How long for tea?'

'Ah, come on Dave. Stop avoiding the subject.'

Begrudgingly, he began to open up about the cancer. He seemed to be focusing simply on getting rid of it. And all the stupid things we were going to do to enjoy life more. He wasn't prepared to show me an ounce of vulnerability. Mind you, I guess he's always been a bit like that. Suppose he's had to be.

'Makes you think, Emma. There's more to sitting in The Angel. I want to do more. Try more.'

'What, like gokarting?' I asked, in all seriousness.

Dave chuckled. Why was that such a silly proposition?

'Dunno about gokarting, Emma. Don't even know where you can do it round here. But we need to have more fun. You pick one and I'll pick one and we'll promise to do both of 'em.'

'OK...' I racked my brain for the perfect activity to cheer us up.

'Well?'

'Shh I'm thinking.'

We sat for a while, slurping our cokes and making a mental library of potential things to do to 'enjoy life'.

For starters, we already had tickets for that Oasis gig, and we'd bagged some tickets to see the Senseless Things at the uni. So that was an easy one. And of course I was going to join him. I had to get my priorities straight, here. Rock 'n' roll is not a cancer. Cancer is. But we did gigs anyway. That couldn't be my special 'enjoy yourself' activity. They were brilliant, but they were the norm.

'What about a trip to India?' I asked.

'Too expensive.' Dave said.

'A bungee jump?'

'Nah, don't fancy walking around with bloodshot eyes.'

'Appearing on The Word?'

'Not sure how we'd wangle that and I'm certainly not

snogging Doreen for the privilege.'

'I've got it.' I proclaimed full of excitement. 'Let's go to Blisters!'

'A roller disco? Emma you seriously want me, aged 27, overweight, with no sense of balance and an extreme dislike of pop music, to go to a roller disco?'

'Yep. You promised. We're going.'

'Fine.'

'So that's a definite then. What's yours?'

'National railway museum.'

'You what? I've known you like, all your entire life, and turns out I'm bezzie mates with a train spotter?'

'Yeah, well. Me dad never took us. Promised me when I was a kid. Never bloody took us. Emma, it's settled.'

'Yeah. Course. Sorry mate.'

Even though we had so much fun together as kids, holidays and stuff, it was always with my dad. You could sometimes forget that, even though we had those trips to the seaside, Dave always had to return home to his unstable family life.

The oven timer dinged, so I stood up and headed to the kitchen. I grabbed the blackened oven gloves from the radiator, pulled open the oven door and found the crispy pancakes were all nice and crispy and the crinkled oven chips perfectly browning on the tips. This'll cheer us both up, I thought.

I plated it all up and took it through to the living room. Dave had put the telly on and was seemingly engrossed in *You've Been Framed*.

He wolfed his minced beef pancakes and chips, whilst laughing a little too loudly at the age-old clips of people falling off rope swings and babies falling asleep into their food. As soon as the credits came on screen he was away into the kitchen with his empty plate before shouting 'right, cheers Emma, got to get off now'.

'Dave, no, we've not talked about…'

'Nowt to talk about there. Other than our trips out. Why focus on the miserable stuff.'

'But surely you need to talk about it. Like, what's going through your mind.'

'What's going through my mind is that I don't want to think about it.'

'But…'

'Got to go. See ya.'

Bollocks.

So much for the bastard mix tape that was still sitting on top of my hi-fi.

Was he in denial? Or did he just really believe that talking about it was a waste of time? I needed to make sure he had everything sorted. I needed to know when his doctor's appointments were going to be. What the surgery involved. I needed to know 100% that he was booked in. That he'd done everything he could. I needed to make sure he hit 28 for fuck's sake.

I was so pre-occupied with why people die and how we might be able to stop it, I didn't think enough about how Dave might feel during the conversation. I was mean. Mean and cruel and selfish.

As Kurt Cobain famously said: 'If you're really a mean person, you're going to come back a fly and eat poop.'

I really didn't want to buzz and eat shit. I'd been very close to that recently after all.

As August hit Hull with all the heat of a typical British summer, I spent an otherwise boring and rainy Sunday poring over my new library books.

Genes and the biology of cancer.

Trends in Cancer Incidence and Mortality.

The Science of Cancer Treatment.

'What you reading there, Emma?' Dad asked. A fair enough question given I'd gone round to see him and, after he made me a cuppa, I'd been sitting in silence reading through my library books – the ones I'd exchanged my rock music biographies for – with a big stinking late fee to boot! Must run in the family!

I lifted my nose from the directory. 'Oh, um. Just doing some research.'

'Cancer? You alright Em?'

'Me? Oh yeah. I'm good. But, Dad. I need to tell you something…'

'What is it?' He had panic in his eyes.

'It's Dave, Dad. He's got cancer? We've got to help him'

Dad took my hands and I explained what Dave was going through.

'Sounds like they've caught it early.'

'Yeah, I know. But we need to make sure he's doing everything he can.'

'He's a big lad Emma. He'll be on it.'

'I know. But Dad. He's 27. And you know what we were talking about when Kurt Cobain died.'

'Yeah. I do. But Dave's not Kurt Cobain.'

'But it's a bit of a coincidence don't you think?'

Dad tried to talk me round. He tried to convince me that just because Dave was 27, it didn't mean he had any less of a chance. It was just a number, he said. But I wasn't convinced. After all my worries, after all my research on the 27 club, after the realisation that maybe it wasn't coming for me, but somebody close to me, Dave gets this cancer diagnosis. How the fuck is that a coincidence? If it is, it's the biggest coincidence I've ever encountered.

Dad gave me a hug and tried to distract me from my books.

'I picked up this Tory rag that someone left behind at Question Time. If you want something to read for a laugh, take your mind off stuff, take a look at this drivel.'

He chucked a previously rolled up copy of 'The Spectator' into my lap. I'd never even heard of it. I thought I better indulge him by flicking through it. Dad stood over my shoulder, obviously keen to flex his political muscles again.

'Him there.' He pointed at the picture of one of the authors, Boris Johnson. 'He's one of the worst.'

I looked at the article entitled: *They seek him here, they seek him there, that damned elusive Mr Blair* – an essay on how the Tories were confused by Labour leader Tony Blair, because they couldn't quite pin him down. He was appealing to the left and appealing to the right. I didn't even know we could have 'centre politics'.

'So what's this about how he might be supportive of a referendum on Europe?' I asked. 'That doesn't sound good?'

Dad went on to explain how the likes of Boris Johnson were keen that we left our European friends behind and became a 'self-centred, arrogant little island' once more.

'What?' I asked feeling really puzzled. 'You mean a referendum where they would ask us to advise them on the things they should be advising us on?'

'Well, it is democracy, I suppose.'

'Well, yeah. But if it works, why break it? And also, how am I supposed to know what leaving Europe would do to us? I'm no expert. Although it sounds frightening, going it alone.'

'I wouldn't worry. It'll never happen. It's just a load of political in-sparring. It's a nonsense. They couldn't ask us to decide on something they probably don't even understand themselves. If Blair got in he'd never do that. And as for the likes of that Johnson prick having a say in anything of importance, I mean, he opens the articles by talking about dropping soap in the bottom of a bath. He's a buffoon, Emma. I'd just ignore him.'

'So why did you give me it to read.'

'Because I think it's important that we understand how the other half live. It gives us something to focus our anger on when we need to vent.'

Fair point. It's better getting our frustrations out on people like that, than on each other. He sounds like a right twerp this Boris character. Thank Christ he's a journalist rather than a politician.

'Fancy another cuppa?'

I held up my mug with a smile and Dad wandered back into the kitchen and put the kettle on, whilst I got my mission back on track and picked up the cancer books.

I was reading all about diet. Apparently, some people believe that green veg is a more effective cure than chemotherapy. I'd no idea if this was true or not but Dave was going to try everything possible. Chemo, surgery, broccoli…

I'd be going easy on the crispy pancakes and crinkle chips in future, I thought.

Dad wandered back through with my cuppa and, as I stood up to grab it, I wobbled and splashed the tea.

'You alright, love?'

'Yeah. I think I've got a blood pressure or iron problem or something.' Perhaps me and Dave both needed broccoli.

'You should see your GP, love. Dave said he was worried about you.'

'Dave did? When?'

'Does it matter. We just think you could do to see your GP. You've been under a lot of stress.'

'Stress? No I haven't. Besides, it's not stress. It's blatantly a diet issue.'

'Whatever you say, love.'

Why did everyone insist I was stressed?

After my millionth cup of tea, I wandered home. Dad said he was going to watch some boring game of snooker on the box so that was enough ammunition to get me off my settled backside.

As I left the house and stopped to make sure the gate was back on its latch, I saw her. Barbara Carpenter. I hadn't seen her in years but she didn't look any less scary than that time she tried to molest my poor Dad under the mistletoe. Her hands were still adorned with great big gold rings and her hair still scraped back off her face with her spiral-permed gelled-to-the-max ringlets hanging out of a scrunchie in a ponytail at the back.

'Hi Emma. Been a while.' She smiled at me. She never smiled.

'Oh, hi, Barbara.'

'Bad news about your mate, Dan.'

So the gossip about Dave was spreading like wildfire and yet they couldn't even get his name right.

'Dave!' I said defiantly correcting her.

'Oh, yeah, sorry. Poor guy. Really hope he's going to be OK.'

Why was Barbara Carpenter apologising? And why was she being so…nice?

'Yeah he will be. I hope.'

She smiled at me again, appearing not to be in any hurry to go anywhere, but with little left to say.

'So…' And then I realised. She wasn't moving anywhere because I was standing in front of Dad's gate. And that was precisely where she was wanting to go.

I eyed her suspiciously. Dad, you sly bastard.

CHAPTER 8

'Aren't you meant to, like, skate in these things, Emma?'

Dave and I were stood in Blisters roller disco. Dave had just finished his fifth circuit and I was hanging onto the side for dear life.

'I don't remember it being this fast though, Dave. The music's not helping either.'

'I thought you loved the Prodigy?'

'I do. But it's the fastest song ever, an' I swear the lights are gonna give me a seizure.'

'Haha, come on, grab a seat old girl.'

We sat at a round plastic table. A foil ashtray spilling over with ciggies and teabags.

I didn't remember it being this bad in here. 'I'm not sure I chose wisely, Dave.'

He laughed as I sat rolling my boots under the table while seated – possibly the only way they were going to get any action at this rate.

'Well, I bet you're looking forward to the National Railway Museum now then!'

'Yeah, well it can't be any worse than this. So, your dad promised to take you then? To the museum?'

'Dad was a right bastard, Emma. I never wanted to talk about it. Because you let it go on so long, and then it's not news anymore. Plus, with everything that happened with your mum and dad...So I just didn't say anything. Then too much time had passed.'

Turns out that the reason Dave never went to the Railway Museum as planned was because his dad had given him a black eye the night before. After that, he was never too keen on going anywhere alone with his dad but it didn't stop him hitting poor Dave. And he wasn't the only one getting a beating in that household, which also explained why his sister, Dawn, left home at such a young age. She couldn't stand the family home. Dave was always getting grief; Dave's mum was trying to drink it away. And Dawn felt completely hopeless.

'I thought she just moved in with her boyfriend?' This was the story Dave had always told me, anyway.

'Yep. She moved in with her crappy boyfriend. Because living with that cheating, lying scumbag was still a far better option that living with Dad.'

I guess all families have their problems. But I couldn't believe all this was going on right under my nose and I had no idea. I saw the bruises, but Dave always said he'd got into a fight down the ten-foot or something. The kids at school were rough as anything, so Dave's story made sense and I never questioned it.

I called Dad about this later on. He knew all about what that household was like. 'Why do you think we always took Dave on holiday with us? It's not like his parents were ever going to book a family holiday.' Dad said. I could hear him munching his way through yet another bag of peanuts whilst we chatted. No doubt he had one eye on Midsomer Murders too.

Everything made so much sense now. Dave's poor mum was drinking day in day out because she couldn't stand the horror of living with Dave's dad. I just thought she was a terrible mother. Seems he was a bully to everyone, Dave's dad. Used to try to control all the money and stop Dave's mum seeing friends. Mum and Dad used to invite them out on double dates but Dave's dad always made an excuse for them not to go.

When I think about it, I never went to play at his when we were kids. At least, very rarely. And that was only when his dad was out at work.

After I put the phone down on Dad, I wandered into the

lounge only to be stopped by the phone ringing. I turned around and picked it up with a sigh.

'Hello 879386.'

'Oh. Hi Emma. It's John'

I wasn't expecting it. It had been ages since he took my number – at least that was how it felt, anyway. I was feeling a little deflated after everything I'd found out about Dave's dad, so I tried to sound a little perkier.

'John, hi.'

After some initial moments of awkwardness and feeling a little flat, we went on to talk for over an hour. He apologised for leaving it so long – he'd had some problems back home with his sister. In some ways, the phone call was a welcome distraction from all the terrible things that had been happening. Was that a good thing? Should I feel guilty about it?

I got to know all about John, thanks, mostly, to the fact he suggested we ask each other questions – quid pro quo, like in Silence of the Lambs - he joked. Seriously, why would a potential love interest want to conjure images of Hannibal Lecter before we've even gone on a date? A slight red flag there. But I decided to let him off – perhaps he was nervous too?

'So, what's the toon like?' I asked.

'Football daft and mourning the underground rave scene' He joked.

'You were never a raver? I thought you loved the Senseless Things?'

'Aye, but you were a nobody if you'd never experienced Rezerection at the Mayfair. You must have some non-indie tunes in your collection. Gan on, what's the cheesiest record you own?'

'Hey Mickey by Toni Basil.'

He laughed. 'You know that's got an edge of old-school cool about it. I don't believe it's your worst. Come on, fess up, what's really your cheesiest?'

I muttered something about Owen Paul's *'My Favourite Waste of Time'* and tried to move the conversation swiftly on. I was perched on the stairs in my big stripy socks and oversized Nirvana t-shirt, with Trevor looking suitably miserable and alone, his head plonked on the floor, sad eyes looking up at me and making the occasional harrumph.

I found myself twirling the cord around my fingers and giggling like a stereotypical girly girl from Beverly Hills 90210 or something. I checked myself and decided to be as serious and nonchalant as I could be, without making him think I hated him.

I asked how Dixie was. She was glowing, apparently. He asked how Trevor was – I explained his poop was, thankfully, no longer glowing.

Things got a little uncomfortable when he asked about my family. I really didn't want to go into the whole thing so just said Mum had left when I was young, and therefore Dad had to take me clothes shopping in Tammy Girl and buy me A-Ha and Adam Ant posters for my birthdays. Poor fella.

I then asked John a question about his family. Turns out he's not had it easy either. His parents were always broke and working ridiculous shifts – his dad, a mechanic, worked all the hours God sent trying to keep his business going. And given his mum was often working late shifts at the bakery, John often had to be both mum *and* dad to his little sister, Jayney, who was five years his junior. He obviously sympathised with my dad given he'd had his own rather embarrassing shopping moments.

'Buying Dr Whites for Jayney when she was 12 wasn't much fun. I had no idea what I was meant to ask for and just kind of awkwardly whispered something about knicker pads for girls to this fit sales assistant behind the counter at Boots. I always went to Superdrug for my Lynx deodorant after that.'

He talked about it all very humorously, but he spoke softly about his parents. He said they tried so hard to make ends meet for the family but they'd got into so much debt that they were always on high alert when anyone knocked loudly at the door.

It turned out that John had adopted Dixie from his mum and dad and brought her from Newcastle to Hull.

'Dad actually brought Dixie home from the pub one night.' John explained. 'I think her owner had passed away and she was part of the house clearance, poor thing. He got her in exchange for a pint and a packet of Embassy No 1. Not sure he had any idea what might be involved in looking after a pedigree dog mind. I could see they were struggling trying to look after her, pay for vet's bills, take her on walks around their awkward shift patterns, so I offered to take her.'

Turns out John got quite attached to Dixie. Taking her for walks with his little sister where he taught Jayney all about birds and wildlife. He loved the outdoors - and I was really loving the sound of him.

Eventually, we wrapped the conversation up and arranged to go for a drink during the week. He let me choose the venue, given Hull was my hometown. I picked the Haworth pub. It was close by, studenty, and pretty chilled during the week.

When date day finally arrived (the wait felt like forever) I was ridiculously nervous. The clock ticked by so slowly at work and I spent all day in a day dream. Until I was jolted out of it by Shane and the sycophant jeering:

'So our Emma's off on a date is she? Who's the lucky fella then? Some goth with problems?'

'Fuck off Shane.' Claire was sticking up for me but I still shot her a look. After all, there was no other way they could know I had a date tonight if it wasn't for Claire. She looked at me with an expression that said '*I don't know what they're talking about. It hasn't come from me.*'

'Hope you're not cooking for him, Emma. We've all seen the state of the lunch you bring to work.' Shane continued and the sycophant fell about laughing.

'What you laughing at, vom features. Never met anyone with such a weak constitution.' Claire added. It shut him up sharp.

I stood up proudly. 'Yes, Shane. I have a date. No, I won't tell you who he is, but I can confirm that no, he isn't a goth with problems. No, I'm not cooking for him we're just having a drink. Nobody has syphilis and no, I haven't decided what I'm going to wear yet. However, I'd be very happy to bring lunch in for you one day if you'd like?' I guess it was my long-winded way of telling him to 'eat shit.'

Shane and his little mate shut their bitchy little mouths and sauntered back through to the sales office. Must have been because I beat him to every possible topic he thought he might embarrass me with.

'Tosser.' Claire muttered, before taking another bite of a Wagon Wheel and another slurp of her tea.

The working day was almost over. We were meeting at 7pm so I had just enough time to rush home from work, walk Trev and grab some tea before pulling on a fresh outfit for our date.

I'd spent the week thinking about what to wear but I still wasn't 100% certain.

I chucked a 60s compilation tape in the ghetto blaster, the batteries still going strong. I hit play and *If 6 Were 9* by Hendrix blasted out. Maybe 27-year-old musical legends weren't the inspiration I was looking for tonight, though. I fast forwarded the tape until it was half way through *White Rabbit* by Jefferson Airplane – one of Dad's favourite songs. I rewound it, fast-forwarded it a little and rewound it again until I found the beginning of the track.

Maybe 60s psychedelia could inform my outfit choice after all?

I threw open my wardrobe and rifled through the selection. Was I going to go for Joplin-esque 60s chic by throwing on my turquoise velvet flares, trainers and love beads? Or was that trying too hard to look suitably cool and chilled, perhaps, when in reality, I was feeling a bit of a nervous wreck.

Maybe I needed clothes that would boost my confidence. Maybe I needed to channel Courtney Love and Kat Bjelland. I hurriedly found my secondhand babydoll dress. Hardly worn, picked up from a secondhand shop whilst on holiday. It was an off-white cotton, with lace across the chest and baby blue ribbon. When I bought it, it was actually below the knees, so I lopped a good few inches off and practiced a little hand sewing. The hem wasn't anywhere near perfect but would anyone really notice? And besides, wasn't that part of the allure?

I threw it on with a pair of white fishnet tights and a heart pendant necklace and stood back to take in the sight.

What was I thinking? This was not the look I should be going for. I liked John. Getting him drunk and into bed wasn't the main aim here. Kinder-whore was not the desired look tonight – whatever kinder-whore meant. I wanted date number two. I wanted to get to the point where we hung out together in our pyjamas. I couldn't channel Courtney Love then. I wouldn't be able to keep up the 'don't mess with me' hardcore sex-queen attitude.

I needed to be Janis Joplin before the feather boas. I just needed to be...me.

Having dumped the previous outfit combinations at the feet of the full-length mirror, I pulled on a fresh pair of Levi's, a pair of old-school Vans, a nice white vest top and some understated beads to add a little feminine touch.

I glanced up at my Athena clock. Shit. I was going to be late. I lobbed a Smacko Trev's way to keep him happy and flew out the front door, praying for the rain to hold off until I got to the safety of the pub.

As I made my way to the entrance, I tried to check my reflection in the window. For once, I was happy with my outfit choices. Understated and comfortable, I had nothing to live up to other than myself. I carefully peered through the window and spied groups of people sitting at the tables near the front and then I noticed him, queuing at the bar. I couldn't believe I was about to spend a few uninterrupted hours with him. John the gorgeous Geordie dog-walker. I mean, the gorgeous Geordie who walked a dog. Although as I had discovered from our phone call, the dog was a Geordie too (despite the name), so I guess you could call him John the gorgeous Geordie who walked a Geordie dog.

This nonsense was a sign that butterflies were fluttering. My brain was going into overdrive. I sincerely hoped the words that came out of my mouth were far more sensible than the thoughts whirring in my head.

As I walked through the door he asked if I wanted a drink from the bar queue with that universal 'want a drink?' hand motion.

In response, I gave him a thumbs up. Fuck. Well, at least his impression of me could only go up from that. He mouthed 'what do you want' and I mouthed back 'sparkling water'.

He looked confused. 'Sorry?' he mouthed.

'Sparkling water.'

Still confused.

I decided to stop trying to be an angel and relax. '*Pint*' I mouthed. He picked his empty glass up and pointed to it as if he were asking for confirmation. I nodded. Thumbs up twice would have been a serious faux pas.

I pointed to an empty table and he nodded in recognition. I made my way over and grabbed a seat while he got the drinks in and then, from nowhere, all the familiar anxious thoughts from those shockingly awkward school romances came flooding back.

Did I change my tampon before I left the house?

I couldn't remember. I rummaged through my bag and saw that I had a fresh one in there. Did that mean I did or I didn't? It wasn't something to take a risk on. My periods had been ultra-heavy since I was a teen. I was always the one with a stack of Tampax Ultra and a load of Dr Whites in my school locker – much to the amusement of the boys.

'Ah look. Emma's got a bucket fanny'.

Oh sweet Jesus. Who would go back to school? And specifically, who would choose to go back to that Geography lesson in school when their period did in fact leak all over their school skirt and the plastic grey chair they were sitting on.

I started to imagine the feeling. I could feel it trickling, I was certain. And in my experience, a trickle can very quickly become a gush.

As John came over to the table with two fresh pints, I stood up quickly and made my excuses.

'Um. Sorry, two ticks. Just need the loo.'

He was obviously going to try and kiss me on the cheek there but I left him hanging.

I nervously started walking quickly towards the loos, realising I'd left my handbag (and therefore stash of tampons) on the table with John and therefore had to turn around, walk back, pick my bag up and…

…well. If you have a spot on your face you tend to think it's easier to point it out before anyone else does. I didn't want him to ask why I picked my bag up (why even would he?) so I quickly said 'erm. Women's stuff. You know.'

Cringe factor strikes again. This is my first proper date with him since meeting, and so far, our conversation had consisted of canine post-coital lock, Trevor's poo and now my monthly period. With a cringey 'thumbs-up' thrown in to boot.

As soon as I got to the loos, I used the few minutes I had to think up some impressive topics of conversation.

Politics? Hmm. Bit early in the proceedings.

Family? I could chat about Dad. But I'd get too angry talking about Mum.

Music? Of course! That's what we had in common. That was not toilet-level conversation.

I strode back to the table feeling pleased with myself. Took my seat and launched into my pre-prepared conversation.

'Seen any good bands lately?'

Could you get a more wooden, more text-book approach to conversation? Luckily, he ran with it, and we got straight into a free-flowing chat (with me feeling much happier knowing that my period was *not* free-flowing) about all the bands we knew, loved and saw live.

What a pair of geeks.

'What's your view on the 27 club?' I asked him, curious to hear his thoughts.

'You mean what they've been saying since Kurt Cobain died?' He asked.

'Yeah. It's strange isn't it. What do you think the common factor is? Other than the age, of course?'

He was far more pragmatic than me. Did this mean we were complementary? Like blue and orange?

'Well'. He said. 'Some rock stars died when they were 27. But some others died when they were 26 or 28. And some are still going into their 70s. I think it's just a headline. What do you think?'

'Yeah. Same.' I lied.

'Although' he added. 'There was that strange tale about that guy doing a deal with the devil to play the guitar…'

'And Jimi Hendrix could apparently play the guitar with his teeth.' I added. 'Also, some say he could play the guitar without even touching it.'

John just smiled at me and offered me another beer.

'I'll go.' I said. He'd bought the first two rounds. No way was he paying for the entire date.

When I wandered back to the table, John clocked my eyes and smiled. This felt so good. It was so relaxed and yet massively exciting at the same time. I smiled and handed him his pint. We launched straight back into conversation, inspired by the tune that was blaring through the pub's speakers – Primal Scream's *Movin' on Up*.

'I love this song.' He said.

'Me too. In fact, I chose it for…'

I cut off mid-sentence. I wasn't sure whether I should be talking about what Dave was going through.

'Chose it for what?'

'Oh, um. My best mate, Dave. He's not well. I've made him a mix tape to cheer him up, you know, because…but then we got distracted chatting and then he left before I had chance to give him it.'

I told John all about Dave. I wondered if they'd get on and I had a sneaking suspicion that they would, which warmed my heart. But it was heart breaking having to tell somebody else about what Dave was going through. It reminded me that it was actually happening. And it reminded me that no matter where I was or what I was doing, I couldn't escape the truth. John was a real superstar though - totally calm and logical about it all but with such warmth.

I must have got pretty choked up at one point, because he reached across the table and grabbed my hand, never losing eye contact. Our first date and I already felt like I wanted him to snog the face off me and be my best friend all at once.

Well. Not my *very* best friend, obviously.

We picked the conversation back up and brought it round to something more light-hearted.

'You'd do what to get on TV? Jesus, Emma. I'm not sure we're compatible. I'm a brown sauce kind of guy.'

Yep, John and Dave would most certainly get on.

When it was time to leave John walked back home with

me. He didn't live too far away, and regardless of whether I needed walking home (I didn't) it was sweet of him to offer and it meant I got more time to spend with him.

As we walked up my street I tried to think of an alternative to the all-too-often-in-the-movies-line of 'well, this is me'.

'Here's mine.' I said, realising it sounded like two kids in the playground swapping a look at each other's 'bits' at breaktime.

We stood outside chatting for a few minutes, and then Trev appeared at the window and started whining.

'Ah, little Romeo's missing his mum, then?' John spotted him first.

I looked over my shoulder and saw his big eyes staring at me, desperate for attention. I turned back at John and smiled.

'I really enjoyed tonight.'

'Me too.'

Our eyes locked and, just as he leant in to kiss me, Trevor starting barking at full volume.

'Let's save it for next time' John said. And kissed me on the cheek.

I couldn't stop smiling. Next time...

I said my goodbyes, he promised to call and I practically skipped to the front door, butterflies raving in my belly.

CHAPTER 9

Over the weeks I spent quite a bit of time with John. We were so relaxed in each other's company. It was lovely.

As I got to know him better, I got softer on him day by day. Every little nugget of information made me weak at the knees. He just seemed like a genuinely decent, caring bloke.

He told me more about his kid sister. When he was younger he'd saved all his pennies to take her away on an adventure-holiday in Wales where they'd go kayaking and abseiling and fencing. He was like the ideal big brother. I guessed it was like how Dave was with me. Bodes well for how thoughtful he might be as a boyfriend.

We chatted on the phone almost daily, shared new music tips, and, eventually, it was time. Time for the big moment. The event we'd both been building up to since that very first day we met.

Dixie gave birth.

I got a call to inform me of the new arrivals. We had five adorable little pups who entered the world in a messy little bundle on John's kitchen floor. Now, there was no way we could avoid the conversation of poo or blood. In fact, we now had to add vomit to the list.

As adorable as they are, puppies can be rather messy.

I took Trevor round to see his missus and his new kids and our little family was simply adorable. Mum (Dixie) looked tired but Trev spent some time with the kids. Licking their heads. Carrying them around delicately.

We were so proud. Equality was alive and well and pooping in John's kitchen (it wasn't just the pups; poor Trev's IBS was flaring back up – must've been the stress of becoming a father).

John's flat was only a short walk from my house. It overlooked the park where I walked Trev and first met John. You could almost forget where you were in that place. We were in the city, but the park was beautiful – surrounded by Victorian homes and trees, a little playpark near the front and an ice-cream hut.

Not surprisingly, his flat was full of beautiful old features. And I'd like to say he complemented them well with soft furnishings and Victoriana. But he didn't. He had a black plastic looking TV stand under his huge TV. A glass coffee table that reminded me of my grandma's house and a stripy duvet on his bed that reminded me of Dave's bedroom circa 1982. But somehow, it made him all the more appealing. He just felt real. Genuine. He loved the same music as me, but he had no pretence about him. He wasn't about to adorn his flat with framed album covers, gig tickets or band t-shirts like some of the music wankers I'd had the misfortune to meet. No, it was his home, not his showcase. And it said a lot about how he spent his time, rather than how he *wanted* people to *think* he spent his time. And I respected that.

A video collection that proudly featured Scarface next to the well-worn boxes of Wayne's World and The Goonies. Copies of the Daily Mirror and Select magazine scattered on the floor. Own-brand shower gel and value loo roll in the bathroom, and yet he hadn't scrimped on the food in the kitchen. He obviously knew how to prioritise. He was a pretty good cook actually. Although we had to eat his seafood spaghetti on our laps with the salt and pepper pots sitting on the crappy glass coffee table.

I loved everything about him.

We actually had our first (proper) kiss in the same spot that we met. In fact, in the very same spot that the pups were conceived. It was perfect. I was wearing a hoodie. We were joking around. I was trying out my Geordie accent on him. He told me it was terrible. He took the tie strings of my hoodie and pulled them, and my face, gently towards him until our lips touched. And he kissed me.

It was perfect. Beautiful.

And it attracted the same teenage jeers that Trev and Dixie did.

'Go on son!'

We just smiled and he held me tight. Looking straight into my eyes with his dark, dark brown eyes. We could have stood there forever.

It really was a moment I wanted to capture and keep hold of. But let's be honest, when people say that they don't really mean it. Because when you have that perfect first kiss, you realise that you want so much more.

Sex. Of course. But not just sex. I wanted to waltz into his house like it was my home too, slip my big cat slippers on and throw my feet up on his sofa for a Friday night of trash telly and takeaway. I wanted to tell him how bad he was at making Yorkshire tea. I wanted him to move his toothbrush into my bathroom. I wanted to see Trev and Dixie having a romantic meal for two together on the kitchen floor…

But going back to the first item on the wish list. Yes. It finally happened. And it was perfect in the most imperfect of ways. No, it wasn't like in the movies - but it *was* wonderful.

We'd had dinner – he'd cooked another high quality meal, although I hadn't been able to tell him that I just couldn't stomach tuna. So, I tried to eat it without letting him see the occasional little retches I was desperately trying to keep in. I got through a lot of beer with that meal trying to wash it down. Reminded me of the time Dave's mum cooked us macaroni cheese and I was practically having a panic attack, wondering how to appear grateful when blatantly wishing that the mushy pile of sick would vanish into the air.

Funny how a little bit of romantic spark in your life can make you feel invincible. Here I was, drinking beer, about to have sex, and not worrying a jot about death for a change.

I tried to make the plate look less full when I was finally defeated by the involuntary retching. I was pushing the food around on it, trying to make it look less, uneaten. He'd gone to so much trouble. He picked the plates up and took them into the kitchen, returning with another beer each before chucking himself back onto the sofa up close to me. We were sipping our beers, sitting side by side, leaning on each other, trying not to be distracted by Terry Christian's thick Mancunian accent on The Word. It wasn't the most romantic of TV shows to have on in the background, but I couldn't stomach the idea of us being one of those couples that clinks wine glasses to the sound of some awful Simply Red ballad. No thanks.

People doing anything to get on TV would have to do. Even if that meant drinking a pint of saltwater, spewing it back up then drinking the vom. The Word was a strange concept.

John was holding eye contact with me more than usual and I became coy.

'What? What?' I was giggling like a shy schoolgirl.

I wasn't usually this shy, but I was so worried about how much I was giving away. This wasn't just about my body, it was about my soul. And there weren't many blokes who managed to penetrate that I can tell you!

But John was. He pulled my legs up onto the sofa and I felt mortified seeing my bright red parrot socks sticking out from under my flared jeans.

I guessed now was the moment to sit the beer down on the coffee table. And I pulled him in close. It was… wonderfully imperfect.

It was wonderful when he tried to unhook my bra and couldn't manage it. It was wonderful when I banged my head on the wall. And it was wonderful when…

Oh my God. I farted. Mid-act. With my stupid parrot socks pointing up towards the sky. I'd left them on in the heat of the moment, which is ironic really because surely if anything was about to kill the heat of the moment it was my stupid red parrot socks.

'Well. That's one awkward relationship milestone out the way.' He laughed. I was glad he saw the funny side. A fart is one thing, but if it was going to let off a stench I wasn't sure I could ever have sex with the man again.

I tried to surreptitiously inhale the air to make sure I hadn't let out some kind of unholy vapour. I couldn't detect anything. Perhaps I'd got away with it this time. Thank fuck I never ate that tuna.

We laughed. We kissed. We picked up where the fart left off. And this time, instead of letting off gas, we both let off fireworks. At least, that's how it felt.

It was perfect. We dozed for a while, holding each other tight on the sofa, until John suggested we head to his room. I was about to climb into his bed for the first time – somehow this felt more of a commitment than the sex. By this point, we were so relaxed with one another, we drifted off snuggling up. After fart-gate, there was no pretence.

The following morning, we stayed in bed all day, drinking his weak tea and taking it in turns to get up and see to the 'kids'.

'That's another awkward relationship milestone out the way.' I joked.

Yes, we were a fully-fledged sickly sweet loved up couple. An actual couple. Except there was no Simply Red ballad in sight.

How the fuck did this happen?

I managed to tear myself away at the end of the best weekend of my life and head back into work. I was going to do nothing to mess this up. I'm not sure I ever felt like this about anyone before.

A dream.

Or as Claire put it when I reported back at work on Monday morning: 'Get the fuck in. You scored girl. I'll have that gift back then now you're sorted. Wink wink.'

There were of course the obligatory questions. The teenage high school sex inquisition. *Did he go down on you? Did you go down on him? Is he pervy, Emma?* But I decided I wasn't going there. I was keeping those fabulous moments all to myself: 'Sorry, Claire. You'll have to use your imagination. Well, perhaps not *your* imagination. Imagine someone less, um, liberal's imagination, perhaps, and use their boundaries to imagine my perfect weekend.'

Not that I wasn't liberal. It's just that Claire had a rather liberal view of what liberal meant.

I was beaming. But it was Monday morning. And we were close to the job opening being ready and waiting. I didn't know what to do. I didn't want to rock the boat with anything. Things were so up in the air at the minute.

I had to prioritise. What was most important to me? My career? Or my men?

Dave had cancer for fuck's sake. I needed to put all my concentration into him. Dad was, seemingly, about to move into some kind of romantic tryst with Hull's scariest woman, Trev was a new father. And then there was John…

Mike called me into his office after lunch.

'Take a seat, Emma.'

I sat on the swivel chair on the near side of his desk. I noticed the orange sponge erupting from the edges of the grey fabric. We might do well selling caravans, but office furniture rarely made it onto our caravan furniture deliveries. Evidently.

He closed the door behind me and took a seat himself. He had a promotional mug from some logistics company half full with black coffee, and rings of the drink imprinted randomly all over his desk pad from where his caffeine hit had dribbled down the side of his mug to form puddles. There was nothing glamorous about the caravan industry. But Mike wasn't so bad.

He went straight in with the burning question: 'So, any thoughts on the role? Joe will be off soon and I need to get someone in place.'

'I. Um. I'm not sure I can accept it. I'm really, *really* chuffed you thought of me for it. But I'm just not sure now is the right time. With so much going on.'

'This isn't about those guys in sales getting jealous and feeling intimidated is it? You'll soon kick them into touch I've no doubt about…'

'No. No. God, no. I'd never let them stop me. They need a kick up the backside the way they go on. No, it's not that. My best friend has cancer. And I just feel I need to be there for him. And I've had puppies.'

'My God, Emma. You are talented!'

'I mean Trev's had puppies.'

'Well, that's just as impressive.'

'I mean. The Afghan Hound he met on the park's had puppies. Remember when I was late because…'

Then I remembered, I told Mike I'd missed the bus that day.

'Anyway. I've just got a lot on. I'm really keen on the role, I just don't know if now's the right time.'

'Look, it's natural to feel nervous about a step in a new direction. We all do. And you've been in the same role since uni…'

'It's not that. I'm so sorry. I would love to take it. I just can't right now. Sorry.'

He looked disappointed. I felt disappointed. I wanted the job. I wanted a way out of the monotony. But you can't have everything? Surely something would have to give? I needed to shut the conversation down before he talked me round. Perhaps I wanted to be talked round?

No. There was too much at stake to shake things up. I had to sustain some form of balance, some form of harmony so I could focus on the priorities. On Dave. On us both making it to 28. And on my new found love life.

I wasn't ready to let anyone I loved leave this mortal planet. I needed to keep my feet on the ground right now and leaving Claire and heading into the new world of sales was a bit daunting what with everything else. And besides, we all know what happened when Janis Joplin left Big Brother and the Holding Company and went it alone. Didn't she predict it in a way, in one of her songs? Didn't she sing about aiming too high and getting burned or something?

Now was not the time to turn my back on Dave. I couldn't think about learning a whole new job right now. And the amount of energy it would take to keep the sales wankers in check was immense. I was exhausted just thinking about it.

I left Mike's office and tried to carry on with my day. Had I done the right thing? It was an especially pertinent question as I was faxing order forms for lavatories. What was I influencing here? Not the number ordered. Not the supplier. Not the product. Not the colour. If robots were going to one day take over the planet, they'd start by taking my job.

John called when I got home. I wanted him to visit my little abode, but what with the puppies we decided it was best I went round to his again. I was relieved I was going to see him tonight. I needed someone to talk to about the job. About my future.

'What if another opportunity doesn't come up, though?' I asked as we sat trying to eat tacos from a homemade kit, spicy tomato sauce and damp lettuce seeping through my fingers. Seriously, who can eat tacos well? Thank God we didn't do this on our first date. Tasty, though.

'Are you sure you can't take it, Emma? Maybe go and speak with him about it tomorrow. Say you're having second thoughts?' John was somehow managing to expertly eat his tacos whilst showing me a great deal of consideration at the same time. I thought men weren't supposed to be able to multi-task? Isn't that what they say? Maybe he's just got magic fingers…

Yes, he certainly does have magic fingers.

Snap out of it Emma. And with that little lapse in concentration…

'Shit! Sorry.'

My taco had instantaneously shape-shifted into about five pieces, spicy beef and tomato splurting out everywhere. Oops. John quickly jumped up and grabbed a tea towel to mop up the Mexican mess, multi-tasking again as he continued to pay an interest in my career predicament. 'Look. If it's really not right for you now, it's not meant to be. The right thing will come along. Something even better. At a time when you're ready to give it your all. You'll see.'

I loved how relaxed we were with each other. I felt like I'd known him forever. We talked late into the night about our hopes and plans. John loved his job, even though, he said, it didn't exactly pay the best wages.

He'd been working in social care for a few years now. The young people in the service he'd been transferred to were all experiencing problems with drugs, alcohol or both. He said it was hard seeing a young 18 or 19-year-old get well and off the drugs and leave the centre, only to return weeks later in an even worse state. The 'revolving door' he called it. Apparently, the number of addicts who stay clean and sober is tiny. No wonder it was so hard for all our rock stars to stay off drink and drugs.

'What do you think drives people to it?' I asked.

'It's got to be some form of a coping mechanism'. John said. And when I thought about it, it kind of rang true. I mean, Dave's mum turned to drink to block out the reality of living with his arsehole of a father.

Maybe sex is the same. Maybe Mum turned to sex with another man to block out…but there was nothing bad to block out. No. That doesn't make sense.

'But why do you think it's so prevalent in rock music.'

'It's so prevalent in many places, Emma. But I guess rock stars kind of become a commodity, don't they? The drugs are part of the allure so why would anybody suggest to them that they need to slow down. They get into trouble because they don't live by the same rules as us 9-5 folk do, and they don't have anyone to help them back out of it. Because, I suppose, for those in the business, they've built a star based on their wild behaviour so why would they go out of their way to help them get squeaky clean. It's tragic, really.'

I guessed he was right. It wasn't just rock stars who lost their lives to drugs and alcohol. And it wasn't just 27-year olds either. John had lost many a young person from the services he worked in over the years. Even in the short time he'd been based in Hull, he said, they lost a young girl, aged just 18, to heroin.

18. I couldn't believe it. Never mind maturing into adulthood – 18 was the very beginning. It was still a transition from childhood.

John's eyes pricked as he spoke. I could see his job could cut him up at times. I was never sure if it was solely the job, or if it was because he worried so much about his sister, Jayney. He often talked about her. She was 23 now and working full time. But he wasn't convinced she was taking the best care of herself.

'Surely, though' I said, without really having any idea what I was talking about, 'Jayney will be fine. I mean, she's holding down a job and everything?'

John explained that Jayney was really bright and passionate about lots of stuff in life, and yet didn't seem to have much regard for herself. When she was 14 she was sniffing liquid gold and smoking spliffs. At 16 it was acid and ecstasy tabs. She was the one everyone wanted to hang out with because she was so much fun – always going one step further than everyone else. Always taking one more pill. He said it was like she had no sense of her own mortality. Either that or she didn't care. This was why he stayed well away from drugs. A beer was all he'd entertain these days.

John said that he felt bad about not protecting Jayney as well as he could when they were growing up. About her hanging out with the wrong crowd. I wondered if this was why he went into the line of work that he did.

'But you were a kid yourself. You couldn't watch her 24/7 – she'd have never thanked you for it' I said, trying to help him see that it wasn't his fault.

He shrugged and moved the conversation onto something a little more light-hearted.

'Fancy some arctic roll and custard then?'

Well, nobody's perfect are they.

I stayed over and Trev followed us to bed this time. Even though he had his little canine family in the kitchen, he sometimes just wanted a human cuddle. It was so sweet that John didn't seem to mind. Although Trev was becoming increasingly jealous of John getting all my affection. He was burrowing his way in between us, trying to make a wedge that he could fall into. The dog looked bloody ridiculous. He was too big and ended up on his back snoring with all four paws pointing up in the air.

Luckily, when I woke up next morning, Trev had decided to curl up on my clothes on the floor, so we managed to get a good night's sleep. I say luckily, but given I hadn't intended to stay over, I was about to head into the office with my only outfit crumpled and covered in Trevor hair.

Back at work, word soon spread about me not taking the promotion. No doubt emanating from the sales guys. A toxic blast of lies…

Claire filled me in on the gossip. Their ponderings were pretty much as expected.

'Maybe they realised she wasn't up to it'

'Maybe she's intimidated by Shane?'

'Think it's cos she's got syphilis?'

And to make matters worse, I was kicking myself when we found out who took my place.

The sycophant. Bri. That nerdy little weasel. That sexist, pathetic Shane wannabe. The sales team's gonna be even more unbearable now. I decided they'd better not find a like-for-like replacement and release another cloud of misogyny into the office atmosphere.

If I didn't see another woman coming into that team I'd be fuming.

But then again, they did try. I said no. I said no because I was too worried about messing up everything going on with the four men in my life (yes, I could now say there were four. Welcome to the gang, John). I felt like the worst kind of feminist.

I settled back into my office chair, picking up the next batch of sales invoices I needed to deal with. Had I done the right thing? Perhaps, instead of taking control of my own destiny, I was letting destiny take control of me? Or at least, letting numerology take control of me.

But Dave had cancer. That, unfortunately, was all too real. If 27 wasn't going to kill him, cancer, in fact, might. It made me feel terrified for him. And if I felt like this, how was Dave feeling?

'Emma can I nab your stapler for a sec'. Shane was marching over with some papers in his hands. Usually, this was a sign he'd made a deal. He had his own stapler, but he would need to be sure that everyone in the office saw the big contract he was about to send through the post.

I decided not to indulge him and just said 'yep' without looking up and he sidled up to my desk, throwing the sales contract on my keyboard so I could do nothing other than look at the big, bold letters: SALE.

Then it struck me. Shit…

I was too late. He already had the drawer open. I let my eyes glance sideways without turning my head, Perhaps I could be surprised that it was there. Like a drug smuggler caught out by a sniffer dog.

Honestly, I had no idea it was there…

The weird thing was, as soon as Mr Sale of the Century saw the Jack Rabbit, he immediately went bright red, shut the drawer and retreated very quickly to the sales office, mumbling a timid thank you.

Funny how some men can be when they don't have their little friends with them.

Better take Jack home tonight. Wonder if I can fit that in my packed lunch box. It's hosted many a suspicious item…

I didn't tell Dave about turning the promotion down. I didn't want him to think it was because of him. I just kind of…never mentioned it again. He had so much more to think about anyway.

'I've got a date through for the surgery, Emma.'

This was obviously a good thing. But it was like everything was hitting home again. Just like it did the first time. This shit was real. And it was all happening in less than a week.

'So that's really good, then?' I said. 'They're getting it sorted out really quickly.'

At that point, I realised that we hadn't really spoken about Dave. We'd spoken about his cancer, his surgery, what might happen. But I'd never actually asked him how *he* was. Dave was always the one I leant on. Looking back, I don't think there ever was a time that he leant on me. Even throughout everything that, as it now transpires, happened in his family home, I never knew. So I never did anything.

Maybe because I never asked.

So now, I promised myself to ask the question.

And I did. We went to the pub. I asked the question.

'How are you *really*?'

Dave said: 'I'm fine.'

Honestly! What was I supposed to do with that? Is it a sign for wanting to move the conversation on? Did he just not want to talk about it? Or was it because he was terrified?

I've known Dave forever. Sometimes I think we know each other better than we know ourselves. So why couldn't I ask a simple question? Why had I let the conversation slip straight back into '*if you had to remove one item from the great British breakfast what would it be?*'

'*Beans*'. I said. I'd never liked beans.

'*Mushrooms*'. Dave said. He'd never liked mushrooms.

We knew all of this already. I can't begin to imagine just how many cooked breakfasts we'd eaten together over the years. I scraped my beans on his plate. He scraped his mushrooms onto mine. We knew all this.

This was banal conversation to fill an awkward gap. It was conversation to try to avoid the real issue. Maybe it was a sign.

So I jumped straight in with it.

'If you had to remove one part of your body what would it be? I'll start. I'd take a boob. Because I've already got two. Your turn?'

He knew exactly what I was trying to say.

'Couldn't I go for a toe. I've got ten of them.' He joked. But then, in a slightly choked up voice he said: 'I'm just not sure I'll feel like a man next week, Emma. I haven't even thought about whether or not I wanted kids until all this came up.'

And I'll be honest, I hadn't even thought of that either. I knew what surgery meant in terms of the immediate risks. But I hadn't considered it might affect his chances of fatherhood. That he might have years of explaining to every new girlfriend what he'd been through aged 27.

In some ways, talking about this was helpful. We were talking about a future beyond cancer. We were talking about Dave turning 28, 29, 30.

'I was reading about this, Dave. Having one of your balls removed doesn't actually mean you'll not be able to be a dad.' I said, pleased with my new-found knowledge.

'Where exactly were you reading that?'

'I got some books from the library. I just, I just wanted to make sure we were doing everything right.'

Dave looked over at me. 'You muppet.' He said softly and smiled. 'You don't need to take all of this on you know.'

'You're my best mate Dave. You're not doing this on your tod.'

There was no way Dave was going to go through this alone. He was going to make it to his 28th birthday. We both were.

I continued to impress him with my knowledge. 'So basically, you might have one less bollock. But, you can still be a Dad. And, when you think about it, you'll be less vulnerable, really, cos there'll be less dangly bits to get hit by the football.'

'Ha, to think that's what I thought the pain might have been.'

'I'm just glad you found it. Me and you mucker, we're partners in crime. We're in this together – like it or not.'

We were on our way to the pub for a bevvy with John and Jayney. That's a real sense of commitment right there. John was introducing me to his sister, and I was introducing him to Dave, who might as well have been my brother.

And anyway, if we were serious then it was time he experienced my little corner of Hull. It's always nerve-wracking introducing a new boyfriend to friends and family. You start to wonder if you've behaved differently with them. Are you like a different person in their company? Do you try to speak differently in their company? Will Dave notice? Will John notice? And will Jayney even like me?

She was coming to stay with John for the week. He'd talked her into it after she'd had a big night out and one of her mates had been arrested for possession. He'd told her she needed to stay out of trouble for a bit. She'd said fine, as long as she could meet his new woman i.e. me. I was equally excited and terrified at the prospect of meeting her.

I needed to brief Dave on exactly what he could and couldn't say. Previous boyfriends were a no-go. Falling off the climbing frame was a no-go. And if he even thought about sharing my biggest most embarrassing secret I would never speak to him again. Cancer or no cancer.

We arrived at the pub early and ordered a half. I figured pacing myself would be a good move – especially given I wanted to be a half decent role model for his sister. Dave decided he needed a pint. And another in quick succession. I don't think it was the anticipation of meeting John, more the anticipation of this week's surgery.

'Be nice won't you, Dave?'

'Emma. I've only ever been difficult when your boyfriends have been cunts.'

'But you've been difficult with every single one of them.'

'I know.'

I was starting to wonder if this was too soon. A mistake. I looked around and something in the pub seemed a little odd. I couldn't put my finger on it.

'Dave. Has Brenda moved some furniture around or something?'

'Not that I know of.' Dave said, looking around. 'But it does feel different in here today.'

Just as I was wondering whether to bring up the impending surgery, John and Jayney walked in.

'Eyes back in, Emma.' Dave mocked.

I was beaming. I was so happy to see him the worry instantly disappeared. I leapt up, went to walk towards him and planted a big kiss on his gorgeous mouth. Knowing it would be inappropriate to linger I pulled away, gave his hand a quick squeeze and said hi to Jayney – with an added apology for slobbering all over her big brother.

She smiled: 'Good to meet you Emma, this one's been raving about you.'

I glanced up at John with a grin – was he blushing? I walked John and Jayney over to our table.

'Dave, meet John. And this is Jayney.'

There was the usual manly shake of the hands, Dave did the same with Jayney (he'd become slightly awkward, I hoped he didn't fancy her). As the football banter about The Tigers and The Magpies (football clubs are like men's names – they always refer to them by something else) got into full swing, I went to the bar to get John and Jayney a drink in. Two pints of lager.

I wandered back to the table with the two bevvies feeling slightly more relaxed and took a seat only to walk in on: 'How was I supposed to know the difference between syphilis and cystitis.'

'Jesus, Dave. I hope you've got it right this time.'

'Yeah. He confirmed you had syphilis.' Jayney said in a serious tone.

I was mortified. 'Dave. No. It was cystitis. They are two completely different things. John, I've never had syph…'

They were all laughing. Roaring with it.

'I'm just kidding with you.' Jayney laughed.

Jayney was really sweet. She had bleached blonde hair and wore a sparkly halterneck top with white jeans. She was definitely not into the Senseless Things like her big bro was.

'So, what music are you into Jayney?'

'Anything really. Well, apart from that shite he listens to.' She said pointing her head at John as she took a swig of her beer. John smiled over at me. 'I mean, like, Future Sound of London, Capella, Shades of Rhythm. I'm always at Rezerection on a Thursday. Bloody love it. You?'

'I'm afraid I'm into all that shite he likes.' I said and nodded towards John.

'Match made in heaven then, eh?' She said and smiled.

We talked for hours. Nothing was forced. No awkward silences. And even my deepest darkest secret didn't deter him.

'You had a crush on David Hasselhoff? Jesus, Emma, what does that say about me?'

I threw Dave a death-stare. It was funny though. Especially when he admitted to having a crush on TV:AM's 'Mad' Lizzie. And when Dave gave me the wink, I knew it meant he wholeheartedly approved. There could even be friendship here.

I could see why John was worried about Jayney. She was often 'nipping to the loo' and I don't think she had cystitis. She would come back noticeably more awake and I could see it pained John. I decided there was no way I was doing any of that shite anymore. I could see what it did to John. And now Dave was unwell, it was time we grew up and looked after ourselves. We were switching from cocaine to broccoli, end of.

Oh God, I hope he's going to be OK, I thought whilst looking up to the ceiling to try to stop the teary wobble. All I could see up there were beer stains, no doubt from an over enthusiastic crowd during a Hull City win or something, focusing on them briefly helped focus my attention away from my worries.

As we were about to leave, I realised what was different about The Angel. What had been missing. And it wasn't the furniture at all.

I clocked one of the old guys, in his raincoat, with his grey straggly hair sitting in his usual seat. Alone. Just a pint in front of him, barely touched, and an unopened newspaper. Where was the other guy?

I stopped to ask Brenda as we were walking past the bar and to the front doors.

'Terribly sad business.' Brenda said. 'The old guy passed last night.' Then she nodded towards the one still sitting. 'His world has changed forever, poor fella.'

'Were they family or something, Bren?'

'Family? No darlin'. They were lovers. They just couldn't allow themselves to be seen as lovers. Been together years those two. I only realised when one of them brought a bag of shopping in – washing powder and stuff. And the other one picked it up as they left the pub. That was a few years

back. Never said a word about it though. It obviously
wasn't something they were outwardly comfortable with.'

All this time and I had no idea. There they were, every
day, reading the papers, drinking the Old Peculiar. I had no
idea that their lives were so complicated. That they had
love and passion but society wouldn't allow them to live
the life they wanted to live. The life they were supposed to
live. It made me think about making the most of it whilst
we were still alive. Why was I spending so much energy
thinking about death?

I thought the old guys were just part of the furniture. I'd
never considered who they might *really* be. I really don't
think I'd ever talked to them. And now it was too late.

'Get me a Drambuie would you, Bren. A little drink for
our old friend.'

Brenda obliged, without charge. And joined me in saying a
final goodbye to a man we all took for granted over the years.

The post family get together de-brief went well. John
called me up the following day to say Jayney really liked
me, despite my taste in music. And Dave called to say he
was happy as Larry for me. That was a first when it came
to my choice in men.

It was only days until Dave's surgery, but the following
night was going to be big, regardless. We needed to make
sure Dave had a cracking night out before his nether
regions became temporarily even more delicate.

Senseless Things were on at Hull Uni Students' Union. It
was like fate. We'd bought the tickets weeks ago,

We met in the Angel absolutely buzzing.

Top five Senseless Things songs?

We always played this game before a gig. If your top five
got played, it meant you were entitled to an after-gig kebab.

After a couple of pints we headed off on our twenty- minute
walk to the SU, walking at great pace due to the excitement and
the fact I needed a wee almost as soon as we set off.

'Syphilis again, Emma?'

'I told you Dave, it's called cystitis!'

He chuckled and winked at me. Cheeky bugger. However, it appeared that perhaps I was having a repeat attack of the cystitis combined with an attack of two pints of lager without a toilet break. As we headed onto campus, I realised I was in serious trouble.

'Jesus, Dave, look at the queue.' I was hopping from leg to leg at this point.

'Surely you can hang on. I'm the one with faulty bits, not you.'

'I've got two full pints of lager to let go of and a recurring bladder infection.'

Yeah. He didn't want any more detail so instead looked resigned to the fact I needed to pee; and nothing was going to stop me.

The queue was snaking all the way down the steps and onto the grass.

'I'm going to ask if I can use the loo'

I left Dave protecting our place in the queue and ran up the steps, getting dirty looks off everyone I hopped by. I made it to the door and grabbed the security guy's sweater.

'Scuse me, can I just quickly use the loo?'

'Think I'm daft. Bloody students. No queue jumping, wait your turn in line.'

'No really – I do need the loo. And I'm not a student.' Not that it should matter, of course. Usually, as a former university student I'd be sticking up for them, but I had more pressing matters on my mind.

He just looked at me and shook his head.

Fuck.

I could feel it. It was right there. The floodgates were ready to open. And this was going to be one hell of a painful exit. Shit.

I quickly scanned the immediate area and decided to leg it round the back of the building near the car park. I spotted a huge holly bush to the right of the queue. It would have to do.

I ran across the lawn, using all my mental might not to grab hold of my crotch to keep the offensive liquid at bay. I headed, as quietly and discreetly as I could, to the back of the bush and managed to balance myself in between the wall and the holly as I crouched with my jeans around my ankles, trying desperately to direct the stream of pee away from my Dr Martens boots. Mind you, they *were* renowned for being able to deal with anything.

The pain was unbearable, like I was trying to force giant razorblades out of a tiny hole. Jesus Christ. My mind flashed back to the climbing frame, split fairy incident and I let out a tiny, pained, squeak.

All of a sudden, my sight was blinded by a searing light. I winced my eyes shut and heard the ground around me crunch as a pair of boots made their way loudly towards me.

Fuck. Fuck. Fuck.

'Oi. You. Step out where I can see you.'

'I. Um. Give me two secs.'

I wiggled around as much as I could to get my pants and jeans back up without being seen, hoping to God that the flow had finally ended.

'Out them bushes. Now!' The light appeared to be moving and egging me to step to the right.

I stepped gingerly towards the light and, just as I was doing up my top button noticed it was a University security guard with a torch.

Shit. Shit. Shit.

'I er...'

'Urinating in public is an offence under the 1985 public order act. What have you got to say?'

This was a campus security guard, not bloody Magnum PI. Jesus. Why was he being so OTT?

'Um. I'm sorry I was desperate.'

'Doesn't matter. If everyone was desperate this place would stink like a public toilet.'

'Inventive metaphor' I muttered under my breath.

He grabbed a pen and notebook from his pocket. Seriously, he was not Columbo or Miss Marple or anyone else for that matter the jumped up little prick. I was feeling angry. Seething, in fact. So God knows where he sourced his next observation: 'You think this is funny?' He was tapping his foot now. Tosser.

I could see some of the queue stragglers wandering by, beginning to point and stare. Giggling was rife.

'Look.' I tried to reason in my most calm and sensible of voices. 'I was desperate for the loo. The queue was huge. The guy on the door wouldn't let me in. I didn't have much choice.'

'Nonsense!'

Good God, this guy was like Mr Bronson from Grange Hill. I could either let him put the fear of God into me, or live my childhood dream and stand up to school's worst teacher. It was do or die. I was already being laughed at. There was no way I was going to be late for the gig. Not for Mr Bronson, not for anyone.

'You.' I said, assertively jabbing my finger towards the security guard's chest. 'have no right to deny me of…of… pissing in a bush.'

'I'll have you know young lady…'

'No. You won't have me know, actually.' I was starting to enjoy myself now. My Criminology degree modules flooding right back to me in droves. 'You're a security guard. Not a copper. And I have a bladder infection.' I couldn't believe how proud I was to say it. 'A particularly bad case of cystitis, in fact'. I continued. 'Nobody would allow me to use the bathroom. I had to use a bush. Imagine how that feels for me, getting my fairy out on the middle of campus. That's discrimination that is. Never mind trying to charge me with a Public Order act for having to resort to a holly bush, where I was in real danger of harming myself, you have no right. I demand an apology.'

'You. Um. Cys…what?'

'Cystitis. I am protected by the law. You must apologise.' Not sure I was being entirely factual at this point, but I seemed to have thrown him off guard.

Our Mr Bronson look-a-like started to shift uncomfortably, head down, muttering something about *'how was I to know'* before retreating backwards into the night.

The queue stragglers were no longer jeering - they were cheering. I'd never felt prouder. I stood, head up, shoulders back and was just about to return to the queue to take my rightful place when I heard clapping from just behind me.

'Nice one.'

A London accent. I didn't know any Londoners. I turned around and oh. My. God.

'You're…you're Cass. You're a Senseless Thing!'

I was beaming. I was also cringing. I'd just been caught with my pants down by the drummer of one of my all-time favourite bands. And he wasn't alone either. There was another guy standing with him.

'Yep. You're coming to the gig then?'

'Yes! I…hang on. You didn't just see me peeing in the holly bush?'

He laughed. Oh my God. The drummer from the Senseless Things saw me pee in the bushes. He heard my cystitis-induced squeak in the bushes. THE Cass Browne heard my tinkle in the bushes. Oh my God.

'Nah. We've just walked up and heard the commotion with that tosser.' He was pointing towards the retreating security guard. 'Gigsy – we got any of that cranberry juice left on the bus?'

I assumed Gigsy was in charge of stuff.

'Yeah, think so. You lot gave up on the mixers last night. I'll go check.'

Gigsy headed off and I was in awe of Cass Browne's knowledge of cystitis cures. 'How'd you know…?'

'Got a girlfriend. I get all this women's stuff.'

Given he must've been in his early twenties, I was

impressed. At least he hadn't confused it with syphilis like Dave.

'Pretty impressive how you dealt with that security wanker. Was all that stuff true? Is having cystitis like a protected characteristic or something?'

'I honestly doubt it. Seemed to believe it though.' I smiled, starting to relax a little.

Gigsy came back with a carton of cranberry juice, which I gratefully accepted a giant swig of. He checked his watch and gave Cass a nudge, I guessed they were late or something.

'Who're you here with then….?

'Just my mate Dave. He's in the queue.'

'Gigsy, chuck us a couple of aftershows.'

What the…I couldn't believe it. After party. As in, we were going to party with Senseless Things. Jesus Christ – Dave wouldn't believe this.

Gigsy handed me a couple of passes.

'Oh God, thank you.' I squealed like an awe-struck teenager. Then shut up to hear his instructions: 'Yeah, just meet us backstage in the dressing room after the gig. Security'll let you by with those. Well…they're not going to mess with you again are they?!'

I wandered back to the queue in a euphoric daze.

'Where the fuck have you been?' Dave was nearing the door now.

'Long story. But look what I've got'

'Well fuck me sideways. How'd you get those?'

'Cass Browne just caught me pissing in a holly bush. Must've impressed him.'

Dave didn't even blink at that revelation, he was too busy pawing over his backstage pass like a kid with a brand new Tonka Truck.

We headed into the SU building feeling like celebrities. Dave got the pints in plastic cups while I dashed to the loos. Oh, thank you cystitis. You've come good this time.

I headed back through the foyer and into the bar, grabbing my plastic pint with no head on it and our adrenaline forced us to down them in seconds. We took our place in the main hall and waited until four, tight-jeaned, t-shirt wearing, scruff-haired pop-punk Gods took to the stage.

They opened with *Everybody's Gone*. We crumpled our plastic pints cups, dropped them to the floor, and po-go'd in sync with the crowd – stopping only for the occasional mid-song rush to the bogs.

They finished with *Too Much Kissing* and when the lights went up, and everyone's face was flushed with sweat and disappointment, we were feeling fabulous. We had a Senseless Things after party to attend. Tonight, we were *with the band*.

After flashing our passes, we were escorted backstage to the dressing rooms. We stood at the door, each urging the other to make the first entrance. Dave looked visibly nervous, so I pushed the door open and tried to muster the confidence of a regular after-party go-er. Dave followed close behind.

'Hiiiiii…' Dave and I rarely spoke in unison. But the sight of Cass Browne with a crate of beers hanging off his arms was a sight to behold. There were about twenty people in there, I counted all four Senseless Things, Gigsy who remedied my cystitis, and a few others who looked like they belonged. Oh God, Emma, be cool.

'Guys, this is Emma and Dan.'

'Dave' I quickly pointed out.

'Ah sorry mate. Come on in, grab a glass of red.'

We settled in, feeling all the more confident after swigging a little Rioja. I'd never seen so many bottles of red wine in one place. I couldn't believe that, just days before Dave's surgery, we were actually hanging out with the actual Senseless Things. It was fate. If anything was going to take his mind off the impending anaesthetic it was the Senseless Things equipped with a red wine anaesthetic.

I got talking to one of the band, Keds, the singer, about finding their vinyl at record fairs (trying desperately to impress) while Dave was offering up his services as a driver to Gigsy (trying desperately to get a new gig on tour.) I felt like all our Christmases had come at once. Dave and I kept looking over at each other, desperately trying not to let our grinning faces betray us.

Eventually, that bloody security guard reared his head again. What did he want now?

'We're locking up now folks. Time to go.'

My heart sank. Such a friendly arse that one. I guessed our time hanging out with The Senseless Things was up. Until…

'To the bus!' Keds stood up and led the way.

Dave grabbed my arm and whispered 'Does he mean us too?'

I shrugged. But decided we should go with the flow and followed them all in line to the bus.

When we got to the car park, I'd never seen anything like it. Plonked in the centre of the otherwise empty concrete space was the Senseless Things' magnificent touring machine. It was the colour of Rioja, fittingly. I hadn't spotted it before when I was lurking behind a bush with my pants down pissing razor blades.

We piled on, and nobody objected, so we assumed the initial invite included us. I had noticed Gigsy refusing a couple of the others on - they must've been professional fan girls and boys. Meanwhile, I was just some Hull girl who got caught short. Maybe that carried more weight. Maybe for the first time in my life, I was cool.

On that note, the first thing I did was ask where the loo was, and was subsequently pointed towards a little bathroom with a note on the door saying 'liquids only'. Thank God I didn't suffer with IBS like our Trev.

After spending a penny, which was far less painful when cushioned with booze, I emerged from the bathroom and my eyes adjusted to the darkness of the bus. It had soft lighting running along the floor, burgundy leather sofas and, although it was hard to be sure given the time of night, apparently blacked out windows.

I guess what happens on the tour bus, stays on the tour bus.

The numerous bottles of red wine had also made their way from the University building, and we set to work draining them, along with numerous packets of cigarettes.

'Lovely place.' I said, immediately feeling slightly embarrassed by my words.

'Yeah. Great for touring. Plenty space for a bevvy or two afterwards too.' Ben the guitarist said.

My mind began imagining the Senseless Things as the mystery guests on Through The Keyhole. *Now who lives in a place like this?* Well, now I'd know. I'd win. Cos I've been invited into their home life. Or at least, their touring home-life anyway.

'Got a ciggie?' Cass asked. Like a Western shoot-out Dave and I both grabbed for our cigarette packets as quickly as we could hoping to be the one to give him a cigarette. Dave beat me.

'Cheers, mate.'

Dave shot me a smug look. I'll give him that one. He's got a difficult week ahead after all.

The music was blaring, bottles of wine were being drained and cigarette smoke was thick as fog. We were in heaven. Tour bus heaven with our punk idols. And for those few moments, we forgot about the cancer and the 27 club. We forgot about work and family problems and money. We forgot about Barbara Carpenter and my dad's intimidating new love life. We felt invincible. Rock 'n' roll made us feel thoroughly invincible.

CHAPTER 10

Ouch. My head was pounding and my mouth felt as rough as a cat's tongue. Covered in sand. And pierced with rusty nails.

Those bloody seagulls. Why couldn't they shut the fuck up and let me sleep. They'd been banging on for what felt like hours. I wasn't ready to open my eyes yet. I pulled the blanket over me and then it struck me. Seagulls? Hull's gulls didn't usually hover over my house. Perhaps we were in for a storm.

I sat up and felt like I was ripping the skin from my arm. I'd been sweating red wine toxins on a leather sofa all night.

I didn't have a leather sofa.

Shit.

I opened my eyes and tried to adjust my twitchy vision enough to focus on where I was.

'Dave. Dave. Wake up. We fell asleep on the tour bus.'

I tried shaking the big lump but he was snoring like a trooper, along with a bunch of other people I vaguely recognised from last night. I figured the band must be tucked up in bed on the top deck.

Heading down the corridor of leather sofas, cigarette butts and red wine bottles, I made my way to the front of the bus and opened the door. Daylight stung my eyes and made me wince. This was no longer the familiar scene of the Hull Uni car park. For starters, I could see the sea.

Feeling ever more confused and hungover I clocked Gigsy heading back to the bus.

'Morning Emma. I've just ordered breakfast – Ian's cooking up a right old feast as we speak.'

'Ah. Lovely. Um. Where are we?'

'Portsmouth, love. Do you not remember?'

'I...no. Portsmouth?'

'Yeah, we've got a gig here tonight. You guys still coming?'

'Shit. Shit.' The blood was draining from my face. This was a matter of emergency. And it sobered me up fast.

'Problem?' Gigsy asked.

'No. Well. Kind of, yeah. Dave's got surgery at Hull Royal first thing tomorrow.'

'Surgery? He OK?'

'He's got ball cancer. They're removing...well...anyway. We can't be in Portsmouth. We need to get to Hull.'

The enormity of the situation was starting to dawn on me and I felt teary. 'I can't believe we've been so bloody stupid. We have to get back to Hull. We've...we've no money. Not enough for a train all the way from Postmouth anyway.'

'Don't you worry. We'll sort something out. Leave it with me.'

I was panicking like mad. Dave was still snoring soundly and it was gone midday. Time wasn't on our side. Christ, how long were we partying for? When did we even set off? I had no idea.

Gigsy put his hand on my shoulder. 'I'll make a few phone calls, Emma. We'll get something sorted. Please don't worry.'

He headed back onto the bus and I followed. Within seconds he'd woken everyone up - including Dave who was scratching his head and farting. Thank God these buses have air con.

'Emma. What's...?' Dave sat up looking increasingly confused as his eyes began to focus.

'Right then folks. Dave 'ere needs to get back to Hull as a matter of urgency.'

Soon you could see the realisation sweep across Dave's face. Shit.

'So we need to work out how we're going to get him there. Anyone know anyone in Portsmouth?'

The realisation turned to terror. Dave was now very much awake.

'We basically need to get him from A to B as a matter of urgency. He's due in surgery tomorrow.'

'Shite. Mate, why don't we see who was playing in Portsmouth last night, see where they're headed?' It was the bassist, Morgan, who'd just wandered downstairs into the lounge.

'Good call. Can someone grab a local listings mag from somewhere will you. I'll try find a phone, call round.'

We sat and waited, feeling sick with worry as Gigsy headed out to find the nearest payphone and someone else I vaguely remembered from last night, Matthew or Malc or someone, hotfooted it to the nearest newsagent to find a listings mag and stock up on everyone's cigarettes. It was coming true, rock music was threatening Dave's life. If we hadn't got wasted on the Senseless Things tour bus, he'd be preparing to hop in a cab to Hull Royal. And he'd have plenty of time for a cuppa and a pasty. Oh hang on a minute, is he even allowed to eat or drink anything at this stage? Nil by mouth and all that. This was all my fault. If I hadn't pissed in a bloody bush none of this would have happened.

The door opened and Gigsy reappeared.

'There's good news and there's bad.' He announced. 'The good news is there's a band who played in town last night who're heading North to Manchester in a few hours.'

'And the bad news?' I asked.

'It's Right Said Fred.'

Oh dear Lord. We were going to spend five or six hours hungover and in the company of Right Said Fred. I guessed they must have played one of those popular student nights where everyone says they're going because it's ironic, but in reality, they just really love singing along to *Deeply Dippy* and *I'm Too Sexy*.

Still, if they could get us to Manchester, we'd be almost home. And just maybe we could afford a train from there to Hull.

We ate some breakfast with the band who wished us well as we headed off to Portsmouth Uni, with Gigsy and Cass leading the way to make sure we got there safely. Nice lads these lot!

The next few hours were the most surreal hours of my life. We boarded another plush touring bus but this time, instead of the tight jeans and punk music, we were chilling out with the Right Said Fred brothers. It was like punk drove us to near death (well, Dave, anyway) and pop was rescuing us.

Or had punk rescued us? After all, we wouldn't have blagged this cushy lift if it wasn't the Senseless Things.

We did toy with the idea of sleeping all the way back, I mean, we weren't desperate to chat to Richard and Fred Fairbrass. But we decided that we needed to challenge Hull's unfriendly reputation by being, well, friendly.

Thing is, pop isn't all it seems. When you look beneath the surface, things can become rather surprising. These guys, the ones who pranced around on stage being Deeply Dippy, the ones who wore mesh vests and black leather waistcoats, well, it turned out they'd performed with Bowie and Mick Jagger. I had no idea cool and cheese could cross boundaries. This was a whole new concept to me. Perhaps the students were right after all…

We were dropped in Manchester, complete with a signed CD each, and we headed straight to the station. It was coming up to 9.30pm and Dave needed to be checked in to the HRI by 7.30 tomorrow morning.

We were starving hungry so made WH Smiths the first port of call. We needed some stodge and pop to keep us going. Then we headed straight to the timetables and grabbed one for Hull. The last train was due in just 10 minutes! Shit.

We legged it to the ticket office. Why was there a queue? Why? At this time on a Tuesday night? Dave's face was white. I knew I had to sort this out. I checked my bank balance at the cash point – I had just enough for both tickets so I drew the lot out and made a dash to the front of the queue.

'Oi, you, get to the back, no queue jumping.' Jesus, story of my life.

'Look Mr. We need your help. I've got to get my mate back to Hull on the last train because he's got surgery tomorrow. For ball cancer.'

'Bollocks' proclaimed the guy behind the desk.

'How dare you!' Said the woman second in line. At first I thought she was talking to me. 'How dare you mock a man with cancer.' She was telling the ticket guy off like a teacher. 'I'll have you know I lost my husband to cancer. It's a terrible disease.'

And that was all it took. The hangover, the stress, my best mate needing his surgery. I stood at the front of the queue and I blubbed like a baby. Big waves of snottiness and tears racing down my face.

Some other guy piped up 'Stop bein' a wanker and let her get her tickets. Prick.'

The ticket guy was bright red – I wasn't sure if he was furious or embarrassed. Dave, rather sensibly, waited outside. What was left of last night's make-up was smudging down my face, and I was close to dropping to my knees in sheer exhaustion and frustration.

'Right. You can buy your tickets, but you better be quick, I've got a queue and your train's leaving in five minutes.'

I was exasperated. 'I know, that's the point.' I blubbed some more.

Eventually we got our tickets and raced to the platform, making it onto the train just as the doors were shutting. Luckily, the train to Hull was quiet, so we just grabbed the nearest seats around a table and recovered the packets of barbecue beef Hula Hoops and cans of full fat coke from our bags. Turns out Dave was allowed to eat and drink up until midnight tonight which was a Godsend given we'd been so stressed we'd not had a chance to eat anything since breakfast.

As the train chugged along, we sat in silence. All we could hear was the sound of us crunching Hula Hoops. I suddenly wished we'd gone for something a little more socially acceptable, like Skips. We were so hungry by this point though the Hula Hoops had no choice but to be loudly devoured. And there was hardly anyone else on the train anyway. I tried to reassure him: 'You'll be alright, you know. And when you wake up, we can tell the Hull Daily Mail that Right Said Fred saved your life. We might even get you in Take a Break magazine.'

I tried to make light of it all; but Dave was clearly anxious. He looked over at me with a half-smile. And I could clearly see the anguish behind it. All of a sudden, my big wonderful best friend, my best friend who always protected me from the shit at school, all of a sudden, he looked small and vulnerable. He wasn't trying to front it out like he usually would. He wasn't cracking jokes to lighten the mood. He was just living the feelings he felt. And I could tell he was really scared. And my heart truly ached. Why, why did this have to happen to my Dave?

'I've just got so many strange thoughts whizzing round my head, Emma.' Dave said, looking me straight in the eye. I don't think he'd really spoken about it honestly before.

'You would have, Dave. I mean, I can't imagine how it must feel. You're being so brave. But you will be fine. You will get through this.' What a cliché. I was trying to be strong, and calm, but inside my guts were cramping up and my mouth felt dry. I couldn't let him know how scared I was that I might lose him. I mustn't let him see that.

'I just, I haven't made any arrangements, you know, in case the worst happens. Like who gets what? I can't have me dad taking everything and selling it. He knows some of my vinyl's worth a bit. And I've not said how I want to be buried have I. Well I don't. Want to be buried that is.'

'Well of course you don't. Because you won't need to be.'

'I need you to know this Emma, it's important. I want to be cremated and have my ashes scattered at Fraisthorpe, but you need to keep a small amount back.'

'What on earth are you talking about. Why Fraisthorpe? And what's with saving some? Not that I even need to think about it, because you're not gonna die. But what do you want me to do with them – smoke them.' I was trying to convince both of us that all would be well. But the truth was, I was so scared I might be losing him.

'Don't be ridiculous.'

I relaxed a little.

'I want Liam Gallagher to smoke them.'

'Jesus, Dave this conversation is ridiculous. You are not going to die. End of.'

'End of. That's exactly what I'm worried about, Emma.'

'Seriously, it's not gonna happen. And how the hell am I going to get Liam Gallagher to smoke your ashes anyway? Rock up to the Adelphi and be like, alright, Liam, have a chuf on this?'

Dave shrugged. I softened and smiled. 'You never told me why Fraisthorpe beach was top of your list anyway? It's nowt special.'

'It is to me. Going there with you guys was the only time I could really relax. Away from me dad. Away from Mum's drinking. Away from that hell hole of a childhood I had. Some of my happiest childhood memories are with you and your dad at that beach.'

I was touched, but it was tinged with real sadness. A bittersweet childhood memory. The only time Dave as a child was happy was when he was away from his family. Well, I guess we were his family. And my Dad loved him to bits too.

It really stood out to me right then just how much we all meant to each other. I mean, I always knew I loved him like a brother. But perhaps we take each other for granted sometimes, you know, because we're just always there for each other. It's like an automatic thing. I get in trouble, Dave sorts it out. Dave gets in trouble, I…panic. I sincerely hoped he couldn't see how worried I was about the cancer. But then again, I needed him to know how much I cared about him.

We spent the rest of the journey in a comfortable silence. Aside from the Hula Hoop munching. And I put my head on his broad shoulder and snoozed as the train sped across West Yorkshire and back towards home. In some ways, maybe our little Portsmouth mishap had done us some good. We got to spend some uninterrupted time together. Me and my best mate.

CHAPTER 11

Other than some vague notion of Catholicism that I picked up when we visited my grandma's, God rest her soul, we never talked about religion in our house. But I knew my Grandma, my mum's mum, was vaguely Catholic. When it suited.

When Mum and Dad went on a romantic break when I was five, I stayed at Grandma's. I remember being devastated that I couldn't go with them on their holiday. Of course, looking back, they were obviously trying to keep their marriage alive. And me living it up with Grandma for a long weekend was one way of giving them the space they needed.

It does seem strange talking about being an only child when; in reality, Dave *was* like a sibling to me. But I was, in fact, officially an only child. So going to Grandma's meant time alone. Just the two of us – generations and, it seemed, worlds apart. But I did get spoilt.

She wasn't strict in many ways, but she was one hell of an assertive woman. I got to eat chocolate, and to stay up late watching the telly with her. And we always got fish 'n' chips if I was there on a Friday (fish cake and chips for me. The potential for bones in a fish fillet always frightened me). But Grandma's inner values were always strong. She certainly wasn't impressed when she found out about Mum's affair. And it was around this time that I first heard the words 'confessional' and 'bad Catholic'.

I had no idea what they meant of course. But from then on, I came to understand that Grandma was vaguely Catholic. Not full time, but it was like a fall-back for times when anyone needed guidance in their lives. Or when anyone needed a firm telling off. Red legs were often made in the name of Catholicism.

'Smacks come to those who do wrong by the Lord.'

Grandma died not long after Mum had the affair. It always made me wonder if the two things were linked. Was it the stress? Was it the family break up? Was it disappointment? Some kind of Catholic shame?

I guess I'd never know. It was filed as cancer but then again, she always said extra marital affairs were a cancer of the modern world. Mum had retorted that Catholicism was a cancer of the modern world. Grandma must have known before we did…

We rarely visited Grandma's for Victoria sponge and orange squash after that showdown.

Just to be safe, what with Dave's surgery in his 27th year and my big birthday coming up, I decided to go with Grandma's take on life and check out the local church. I simply *had* to do something. I certainly couldn't sit at home, twiddling my thumbs waiting for the news while Dave was under a general anaesthetic. Grandma might have eaten more chips than Mum but there was certainly something more spiritually wholesome about her.

When it came to religion, having only been to a couple of services with Grandma as a kid, I had no idea what I was supposed to do. Was it a club you had to formally sign up to? Could you just rock up, take a pew, pray on your knees and enjoy a new life of wholesome goodness? The only way to find out was, in fact, to rock up.

I decided to get my wardrobe in shape first of all though. I still had my 1980s jewellery from Madonna's *Like A Virgin* era (I might love rock music but nobody and I mean *nobody* avoided the Madonna craze in college. I think we even had Dave in fingerless lace gloves at one point). I replaced my tiny silver sleepers with my cross earrings from Saturday market, and teamed them with a polo neck jumper to look refined. It had glittery stripes across the front but I figured it was conservative enough for church given it was trying to strangle me with shame. Besides, Christmas was a religious festival and look how glittery that is.

I knew there was a Catholic church a few streets away - about a fifteen-minute walk from home. And my God, I needed to take my mind off the fact that my Dave was in hospital waiting for his operation.

I'd never really paid any attention to the church before, other than noticing the banners on the side of the building, inviting us all in off the streets for a spiritual hug with God and His Son. I always felt it was a little pervy, to be honest.

As I wandered down the street my head was contemplating the scene that lay ahead. Golden leaves can make any street look beautiful. Even the ones lined with 'Happy Shoppers' and 'Booze Busters'.

I approached the church and the doors looked open, so I headed in tentatively. Wandering in, I realised that the last time I'd been in a church was Halloween night circa 1977 or 78. Myself, Dave and a couple of the kids who lived on the same street decided it was the place to try and conjure the dead. We had ideas of strange looking ghouls rising up from the pews and coming at us like something out of The Omen.

We truly believed there was something very frightening in there. A sense of doom. A sense of panic. You really can make yourself believe anything when you egg each other on.

But unfortunately for us, the reality was far more frightening than the imagination. There were no spooks, ghouls or zombies. But there was Mrs Hillier from the school library. And we were severely reprimanded for bringing a bunch of Scrabble letters in a sandwich bag into such a holy place to conduct such unholy business.

What is it with me and unholy sandwich bags containing unholy doings?

Our makeshift Ouija board never did make contact with the other side. But Mrs Hillier's hardcover bible made contact with Dave's backside as we sprinted down the aisle and out the front door.

Talk about bible bashing.

But that was then, and this is now. I had a holier reason to visit this time – I was entitled to be here whether Mrs Hillier liked it or not. So, with a renewed sense of wisdom, I walked into the building and was hit with an overwhelming silence. My footsteps were echoing and my clothes were shuffling. I could even hear the jangle of my crucifix earrings. But even though the building was cold, I felt a warmth as I walked down the aisle towards the altar. I had no idea what I was meant to be doing there, so I decided to take a pew and see if I might be overcome with some kind of spiritual guiding force.

Sitting on the cold wooden bench, two rows back from the front I took in the smell and the stained-glass windows and felt strangely at home in such a mysterious, cavernous and yet beautiful place. I closed my eyes and sat for a moment. Thinking about Dave, thinking about Dad and all that business with Mum. Thinking about how lucky I was to have Trev. And thinking about John. Those eyes. That first kiss. That first time in bed…those magic fingers… then a voice came from nowhere.

'Are you here for confession?'

Oh my God! The Lord knew. He was here, all around, just like they said. Just like in the hymns. I spoke and He heard me. Straight from my mind. My dirty, disgraceful mind that was thinking sinful thoughts in a holy place. Thoughts about sex before marriage.

I failed on my commitment to celibacy until marriage.

I failed on innocence.

He'll know about everything. He can read my mind. He'll strike me with a 27 club death because I thoroughly deserve it.

I felt like a tainted demon trespassing on holy ground.

No wonder people who go to church believe in all this magic stuff. I'd been there for precisely three minutes and I had accidentally summoned his spirit. His guidance. Or his penance. I'd have to wait and see what lay in store for me.

I kept my eyes shut tight. And I replied. Out loud. I spoke directly to Him.

I knew the right words. I'd heard them on the telly.

'Bless me father for I have sinned.' I said.

'It's OK. If you're here for confessional, you can talk about it.'

I recognised the accent. God was a Hull bloke.

'I have been sitting here in this holy place thinking dirty thoughts, Father.'

'Open your eyes if you like, love' He said. How very informal I thought.

I did as He said. I opened my eyes and there He was. Standing in front of me with a smile on his face. Like an angel glowing in his white robe, back lit by a beautiful stained-glass window.

'Hello.' He said.

'Fuuuuuuccccckkking hell…' I muttered under my breath. 'Sorry, Lord.' I added more audibly.

And then I did the sign of the cross over my chest.

The Lord giggled. He held out His right hand.

'Hello dear. I'm Father William. The priest.'

Fuck's sake Emma, are you on fucking glue. He's the bloody priest. Of course he's the bloody priest. He's not God. God does not have a Hull accent. He'd speak in the Queen's good and proper English.

'Of course you're the priest.' I stuttered. 'I know you are the priest.'

Who was I trying to convince?

'Are you here for confessional?' he asked.

And I decided, seeing as I had resurrected my 1980s crucifix earrings for this very special outing, I shouldn't waste them. I should confess. That's about as far removed from making a deal with the devil as you can get. If anything was going to prolong mine and Dave's life, and with that, our friendship, this would be it.

'Yes, Father.'

He led me to the confessional and I took my seat. I started from the beginning. I knew the opening line. I imagined I just needed to pour it all out from that.

'Bless me father for I have sinned.' I waited. Nothing. Silence. Should I carry on? I decided I had nothing to lose. Maybe this wasn't like an interview. I should just...confess.

'Um. Obviously, my most recent sin was a few seconds ago, sitting in a Catholic church that I'd never been to before, thinking about having sex with my new boyfriend. I guess that's where I should start. So, I'm sorry about that just before. It just crept into my mind because he's really nice and I haven't had a proper boyfriend in a long time. And I think it might be love, so I wonder if that makes it OK? Or at the very least, slightly less sinful. Perhaps I can save some sin tokens given how much I care about him. Does that work? Hehe.' I let out an awkward giggle.

Silence.

'Erm. I've been here before. Just not for confession or anything. I brought a makeshift Ouija board in. With my best mate Dave...'

And then it kind of just...spilled out.

'He's got cancer. Dave has. My best mate. And I just don't know how to deal with it. When Kurt Cobain, who you probably don't know, but he was in this mint band called Nirvana, well when he died in April... he was 27. And I'm 27 soon. Dave is 27 now. And I'm just so scared because things always seem to happen to people I love. Bands, friends – best friends - family. I feel like I must be doing something. Something to cause all this. It's too much of a coincidence but I can't lose him. I can't lose my best friend. I just don't know how to stop it. How can I stop it? Is it about the music? Is there something to do with rock music? Mum and Dad loved it too. And look what happened to them. Am I losing it Father? Cos I just can't understand why so many people are, you know, leaving me.'

It was quiet. Was he still in there? I hoped I hadn't passed all my toxic badness onto the priest and killed him instead. I sat quietly, allowing my breathing to slow down following my huge outpouring. My hands were full of pins and needles again.

Then came a voice. 'I quite like Nirvana, actually.' He said.

'You do?'

'I do. Good music transcends age. But why would you think rock music is the work of the Devil?'

'Well, sometimes they sing about Satan and bad stuff happening and there was that whole bat incident with Ozzy Osborne...'

'Yep. But in the Church, we read about Satan as well as God. There are good and bad forces in the Bible you know. And everything in between. It'd be a pretty boring story if everyone just hung out together eating fish and drinking wine all day. Well...on second thoughts...'

'So you're saying rock music isn't bad?'

'Oh not at all. Some of it's dreadful. You'll never catch me ironing my cassock to a Megadeath CD. But the people who create it, they're just people, expressing the good and bad stuff in life. Just like the Bible does. Except their lyrics are a tad more...liberal.'

'Why do they keep dying then? What do they have in common? Why did Dave get cancer when he was 27?' I asked. I assumed priests knew the answer to everything. Although, wasn't the answer to everything in the universe supposed to be 42? So why did the number 27 keep cropping up?

Then Father William asked me to think about time. He asked me to think of a year I had lived through and then to consider what happened in that year. I chose 1986.

1986 was the year that Madonna cut her hair short. It was the year that I got my university offer. It was the year that idiot ex-boyfriend, Danny, treated me like shit. It was the year that one of the greatest movies ever made – Ferris Bueller's Day Off – hit the cinemas. And it was the year of Halley's Comet. But it was also the year that Chernobyl exploded.

'So in that one year, loads of good and loads of bad things happened. How old were you?'

'18' I answered.

'And now you're 26. Some good stuff is happening. And some bad stuff is happening. It doesn't have to be black and white. It's not about life or death. Really, it's just about life. This is life and it's throwing things at you. And you don't have to choose between them. Just experience them. And do what you think is best. Don't argue with yourself about what you should and shouldn't do. You can't control your friend's health. Go with your gut feeling. There's rarely an answer in life. Regardless of what the Hitchhiker's Guide to the Galaxy told us. 27, 42. They're just numbers.'

It made some sense.

'I've never really thought of it like that, Father.'

'It can be difficult to separate logic from emotions. Often, we create our own idea of logic to fit our emotions. Somehow it's easier, even though often, it's more painful once you've reached whatever conclusion your emotions are leading you towards.'

'You mean my worry has created the logic behind the curse of the 27 club?' I asked.

'Well, I think it was more of a cumulative effort to be honest. The media didn't help either. All these conspiracy theorists.'

I was beginning to feel more relaxed. I thanked him and stood up to leave. But before I left…I needed him to know I hadn't spoken with the Devil in church…we were not in cahoots.

'In case you were wondering, Father. We never actually used that Ouija board. Mrs Hillier from the school library caught us carrying the scrabble letters in a sandwich bag and chased us out with a hard-backed bible.'

'Good.' Said Father William. 'We might talk about the Devil in church. But we certainly don't invite him in for a cuppa.'

I was just walking back down the aisle when he added: 'Just one last thing. Kurt Cobain took his own life because of his inner conflict and pain. Inner conflict is far more dangerous than a birthday. Make sure you talk to someone, won't you?'

I nodded, confused, but smiled and then slowly walked out the church.

Was he saying I had inner conflict? Inner pain? I'd always wanted it in art class as a teenager. I remember telling Miss I'd never be any good at Art because I wasn't tortured enough. Maybe I was wrong. Maybe something had been twisting in my guts for a long time, unable to breathe the cold air and rise up and out of me. I'd been sad for a long time really. Sad and angry at Mum. Upset that she cheated. Angry that she left us.

Heading back home I decided not to see John that evening as planned. My head was spinning with too many thoughts and it was early days in our relationship so I didn't want to land a heap of emotional baggage on him. There were angry thoughts about Mum bubbling up, anxious thoughts about Dave screaming in my head. I didn't feel like I should be sat having fun, giggling, snogging the face off someone when I had a whirling dervish of terror in my head.

Besides, I needed to be by the phone in case Dave or the hospital rang.

I decided to read up on Kurt Cobain, thinking about what Father William had said. I pulled out my old music magazines from under the bed and flicked through them until I found a copy of Rolling Stone from January and an NME from last year – both featuring Kurt on the cover.

I pulled my pyjamas on and headed back downstairs, magazines tucked under my arm and Trevor following at my heels. In preparation for my research I made myself a nice cuppa and carefully placed an entire packet of malted milk biscuits within easy reach of the sofa.

I scanned the Rolling Stone interview – even though I had no doubt already read it hundreds of times over. But to re-read it with Father William's comments in mind was interesting. Kurt Cobain talked of his stomach problem and the pain he tried to tame with heroin. He talked about being a dad, about having no more songs in him, and he hinted that there may not be a future for Nirvana. He talked of owning guns, why he had them in the house, to protect himself and to go out shooting in the woods for fun.

I tried to translate his problems into a Hull world. Maybe that's what it would feel like to think you could lose your job at any moment, or to feel unsafe in your own home, or to have no more inspiration left in you so that your world becomes apathetic and in desperate need of something, anything to free you from the monotony. And then, of course, if you chuck a shit load of physical pain on top of it all you might get somewhere close to what Kurt Cobain was feeling.

I picked up the copy of NME from the year before and reviewed its words. It's weird reading them both now, Kurt Cobain talking about how happy and content he is in 1993, and all the pain and anxiety in 1994. The NME interviewer even commented on how happy and content Kurt Cobain seemed. And they discussed the fact that his song '*I hate myself and I want to die*' was meant to be a joke. A joke? And yet months later…

So I guess if there was a heap of pain and turmoil inside, and I'm not just talking about his stomach here, maybe he kept it well hidden. We knew plenty from the music, but maybe he didn't even admit to himself that he was mentally tortured? Or maybe he just didn't admit it to the world – after all, we might have all been fans, but we were strangers at the end of the day. We've no idea what really caused Kurt Cobain's death. What really drove him to suicide. But I was beginning to think there was far more to it than a number.

It can't have been easy to be happy and content one minute and pained and conflicted the next. Just like that day Mum left. My world changed in a mere moment. A day where everything else around me was carrying on as normal. The kids were playing British Bulldog out in the street and telling any gate-crashers to '*fuck off or I'll brae yer*'. The telly was on in the living room, the sound of snooker balls knocking into one another in a patient and considered fashion, the occasional controlled applause from the otherwise seemingly sedate audience. The sound of Jimmy next door sawing wood in the front garden, sawdust everywhere, can of Labbatt beer on the ground by his feet and the radio on, mingling awkwardly with the sophisticated sounds of snooker. I remember it all. All the insignificant goings on. And all of those sounds – the snooker, the sawing, the kids playing, the Labbatts, David 'Kid' Jensen's voice on the radio - they still make my stomach flinch and my nausea rise if I ever come across them. Why was that?

Maybe Kurt felt that the only way of removing that inner pain – those triggers - was to exterminate them all in their entirety. And let's be honest, with no songs left in him, guns in the house, a history of heroin addiction, excruciating pain – not many stars would need to align to create the perfect time to die. Perhaps the 27 club wasn't a curse or even a coincidence, perhaps 27 years is just too long to have built up a heap of emotional pain and baggage without turning on the tap and releasing some of the pressure. Bang. All gone.

Maybe rock music was more a coping mechanism than a cause.

I guessed I also needed to release some of the pressure. Some of the simmering emotions that I kept locked away. I knew I didn't want to die, that went without saying, especially given how I'd spent so long worrying in case I might. So, maybe I needed to find another way – a healthier way – of turning on the tap.

Father William was right, those thoughts had to come out. I needed to talk to someone.

'Can I talk to you, Trev?' I asked as I curled up with my faithful friend that night. He harrumphed in response.

CHAPTER 12

The smell of hospital food wafted all around me. Minced beef cobbler. Chicken pie. Something like that. A kind of school dinner sort of smell. Machines were beeping like an out-of-harmony choir and people were rushing around as if life depended on it.

Life did depend on it.

I looked over at Dave. He was smiling.

'Are you OK?' I asked him.

'Of course. I'm still here aren't I? At least 90% of me is anyway.'

'Is that the percentage of ball to man then? 10%. I fear my boobs make up a relatively smaller percentage of me.'

'Yeah. I'm just trying to make myself feel better. The more I've lost - the more man I was. It's probably more like 1% to be fair. So probs won't make much difference…'

'They told you anything? Since last time we spoke?'

'It's still all looking good Emma. I'm still heading in the right direction. I mean, I'll live. But not sure my offspring ever will. But one day at a time, eh. Besides, I think Trev's doing quite nicely in growing the family. How's John?'

'He's good. He and Jayney really enjoyed meeting you. Said to pass on his best and that he's looking forward to a pint when you're up and about again.'

'We better get a date in the diary then, cos it won't be long. I'm out later today, just waiting for a check-up then I'm a free man. Not allowed to drive for a while though. Which means time off work.' He winked at me.

It seemed like such a quick turnaround for something that can cause so much destruction. Cancer – gone in one fell swoop. Hopefully. And a bollock too. When I thought about it, the two cats we had when I was a kid both went to get neutered at the same time. The tom was chasing his tail and wolfing down his biscuits within five minutes of coming back home. The little girl on the other hand came home with a cone round her neck, wobbly on her feet and feeling and looking thoroughly miserable. And Dave's only had one ball off. So I reckon he'll spring back just like our tomcat did.

'Ooh, I've got something for you.' I pulled the mix tape from my bag and handed it to him. 'I made it when you first told me about the cancer. It's probably a bit soppy.'

Dave studied the track listings carefully. 'Nowt soppy on here. Top mix tape Emma, thanks!'

'Alright, mate. How's it going?' Dad's head appeared from around the curtain, with a plastic Jackson's bag dangling by his feet. 'Got you something.'

'Well, the Barclays are certainly making it feel like Christmas round here. I should book in for another bollock extraction soon.'

Dad chuckled and handed him the carrier bag. 'Nothing special I'm afraid.'

Dave greedily tucked into the bag, pulling out the token grapes, a Pot Noodle, a copy of Loaded magazine and a multipack of Snickers bars.

'Thought you could do with more nuts.' Dad joked. I shot him a look, but Dave just laughed.

'Aye, you're probably right there, Tel.'

'How they treating you then?' Dad asked. 'How's the food.'

'Ah that all-important question.' I smiled. 'Smells like school dinners in here.'

'I wish it was' Dave said, holding his Pot Noodle and visibly trying to suss out where there might be a kettle. 'There's no marble sponge and pink custard in this place, sadly.'

'That takes me back.' I laughed. Dave and I were two of

the few kids who actually enjoyed school dinners. Except the chicken pie which made me retch. And the semolina. But give me a cheddar buttery with chips and beans any day.

'On the subject of scran, I better go and sort Trev out, he'll be starving.' I got up to leave, kissed Dad and gave Dave a big hug.

'Thanks again for the tape, Emma. Love it.'

'Glad you like it. See you in the pub, then.'

Trev was pleased to see me when I got home, the little whippet was all over me – jumping up and down as if he hadn't seen me in weeks. I'd like to think it was part of the whole 'man's best friend' relationship thing, but I had a sneaking suspicion he was just really hungry.

I'd already cooked some chicken breast so I plated some up for him from the fridge and grabbed myself a cold can of Oranjeboom.

I'd been thinking about the church. The impromptu meeting with Father William. The 60-odd—year-old Nirvana fan with an impressive knowledge of rock music. But on a serious note, what he said was interesting. All this time I'd been searching for the answer. Trying to find out what it is that kills us when we're 27.

And yet Father William said it was the inner turmoil. Not the number. Not the music. Not the lack of innocence or the cigarettes or alcohol (they do of course kill us, but not necessarily at 27). And certainly not the devil. It's the shit that lives in our head that's so dangerous.

What was in my head? As far as I could tell it was made up of Trev, Dave, John and Dad, and it was kept pretty busy with all their shenanigans. Sure, I was a bit angry at Mum still, and maybe that was just normal. Or maybe it wasn't?

I booked an appointment with my GP. Dad had been nagging me to go anyway, to talk about my 'fainting spells' as he called them. Even though I'd never actually hit the deck, I guessed they were a bit bothersome. And after seeing the Priest, I wondered what he meant about talking to someone. A doctor, perhaps? Stress, maybe?

I managed to get an appointment for that week.

I sat fidgeting in the waiting room, reading an old issue of Cosmopolitan magazine. Disappointed by the fashion I was desperate to just get this blummin' appointment out the way. I hated going for medical appointments. It was 8.30am though, which meant I wouldn't be too late for work.

I looked over at the old lady coughing into a tissue with shaky hands, clearly ridding her lungs of whatever it was that shouldn't have been in there. Pneumonia maybe? The appointment board pinged and I perked up, only to be disappointed when the name read Arthur Smith rather than Emma Barclay.

A bloke around the same age as my dad stood up and hobbled along to the corridor in search of room 12. He was on crutches and his foot was in plaster.

Broken ankles and pneumonia. They were real reasons for seeing the doctor. Perhaps I shouldn't be here. You know, just for getting a bit wobbly sometimes. I put the magazine down and stood up ready to make my exit, only for the appointment board to spring to life with my name.

'Emma Barclay. Room 6.'

Well, it would be rude not to.

I gingerly knocked on the door of room six before entering and sat down in front of the locum. In some ways I was pleased when they said Dr Anderson wasn't going to be in today. I'd known him forever; it would have felt odd talking to him about feelings and stuff. He knew my mum for starters.

'Hello, Emma. How can I help you. Do take a seat.'

The locum, Dr Yagnik, was a smiley lady. She didn't look much older than me in all honesty. Why is it we think doctors can never be the same age as us? It's as though you're judging them on everything you've not achieved by now, rather than remembering that some people did work their socks off and launch a career in their chosen field. Besides, I guess younger doctors have sharper brains. Or is that ageist?

My brain was racing again...

I sat down and Dr Yagnik continued to smile at me, but I said nothing. I was as mute as an instrumental on a 7" B-side. Why did we get instrumentals anyway?

She raised her eyebrows, pointed her head forwards and said 'so…what can I do for you, Emma?'

'I um. There's two issues actually. I've been having these strange spells. Like, feeling faint and getting pins and needles.'

'OK.' She said. Any other symptoms.

'My heart races too quickly sometimes. And I feel breathless.'

'And how long does this last? Does it come and go?'

'Yeah. It just comes on, out of the blue. One time I was walking along and literally had to sit on the ground, I was so faint.'

'And your other problem?'

'I'm not sure it's a problem. It's just, I saw the local priest, and he said I needed to speak to someone. And I wondered if he meant a doctor?' I explained all about my 27 club obsession. Dave's cancer, the conflicting feelings I had about Mum, my concerns for Dad.

'It sounds like you've got a lot of unresolved feelings about your family. And the thought of losing someone close to you must be stressful. Plus, the physical sensations you've been experiencing…I think they could be panic attacks.'

'Panic attacks?'

'Yes. If you've been experiencing a lot of emotional anguish, it could account for why things have got bad lately.'

'But how do my emotions, my thoughts, have an impact on my heart and my balance? I thought I'd just need to eat more broccoli or something.'

'I can't comment on your diet, Emma. But your brain is a powerful thing. It can have all kinds of physical impacts. I think we maybe should consider counselling. I think it could be helpful.'

'What, like a therapist? Like on TV?'

Dr Yagnik laughed. 'It's nothing like the telly, don't worry.'

'I'm a bit embarrassed to be honest'. I said. 'Shouldn't I be able to just chat about this stuff to my mates?'

'Well, I suppose it's difficult sometimes, to have really honest and open conversations with people who are close to you. Maybe there are things you might hold back. With a counsellor, you won't have those worries. You won't need to be careful with what you say. Plus, it's highly confidential.'

I felt reassured. And agreed to be put on the list for an appointment.

It seemed I'd left the surgery just at the right time, as the bus was pulling into the stop outside as I approached. I ran over and jumped on just in time, feeling pleased with myself that, for a change, the day was running rather smoothly.

I got to work for 09:15 which wasn't bad going at all. Still didn't stop Shane from tutting and tapping his watch when I walked through the door.

'Doctor's appointment' I said, justifying my lateness with confidence. He walked off with his head down.

'Ha!' Claire was laughing. 'He probably thinks it was a follow up appointment to the ole syphilis business. They get embarrassed these men.'

'Cept I never had syph...oh whatever. I don't really care what that twat thinks anyway.'

'Seriously though, Emma, all OK?' Claire was genuinely concerned, I could tell. She had that same look on her face as she did when I suggested I might become celibate.

I didn't want to open up a can of worms so I just told her it was all good – just routine stuff.

When I got home I had an answerphone message from the counselling service. They had an appointment for this week – somebody had cancelled so it had opened up last minute. I was to call back by tomorrow lunchtime to confirm.

I knew I had to take it, but it felt nerve-wracking. I'd never done anything like this before. I needed a night of chilling out with a pizza and a bottle of beer. I called John and we decided to grab a movie from the video shop. He didn't have a card, so I said we'd use mine…

Oh God, the video shop! What with all the love in the air I'd forgotten about that wet pussy! Which is ironic, really.

I just had to pray that the same girl wasn't on behind the counter.

The same girl was on behind the counter.

Oh shit.

We had a nosey through the 'new in' videos. You can tell a lot by somebody's taste in films. What was John likely to go for I wondered…?

Would he drift over to the classics in a bid to impress me by suggesting we get Breakfast at Tiffany's out? Nah – he's too authentic. He wouldn't waste his time pretending to like something just for me. As much as I could have watched the movie a hundred times over with Audrey Hepburn and her cat…

I said cat. Not pussy!

I shook my head trying to dispel the imagery that refused to leave me be.

'What about Natural Born Killers, you seen that?' he said?

Hmm. He was playing it safe here. Natural Born Killers is a movie that nobody can diss. Shame I'd already seen it though.

'Sorry, John. Me and Dave watched it as soon as it came out. He had it reserved for about three weeks before it arrived in the shop!'

Lucy Nichol

'Dumb and Dumber?'

Aha. He was letting his guard down now. He was obviously relaxed with me. You'd never suggest Dumb and Dumber on a first date would you? I mean. It's embarrassing. We were obviously connecting at a deeper level now, hence why he suggested something so despicably shallow. Because he doesn't care. Bonus points for John. Except there's no way I'm watching that shite.

'Hmm…don't really fancy it.'

'Pulp Fiction?'

'Yes!' I replied, excitedly. 'I've been meaning to watch that for ages!'

'Give us your card then, I'll go and pay for it. I'll grab a tub of Haagen-Dazs too.'

I handed over my card and idly traipsed behind John, after regretfully eyeing up the new Flintstones video. I'd have to watch that with Dave or Dad sometime.

'So, Mr Barclay I take it?' the girl behind the counter asked. But before I could step in, John decided to take on the role, answering loudly and proudly with, 'aye, that's me'

The grumpy cow started sniggering. Why was it that the only thing that drew a smile in this girl was my embarrassment?

John looked slightly perplexed. And then she followed up with: 'You'll be pleased to know your wife took care of that little business of your late fee.'

'Oh, yes. Thanks, love.' John said, playing along with it and winking at me.

'So would you recommend 9 Lives of a Wet Pussy Then?'

'I, er…'

My face must have gone as red as a beetroot. From the embarrassment in front of John, and the anger towards this jumped up video shop assistant. The cow!

'Right, OK. How much?' I asked frantically. Desperate to get out of the shop and flitting through my purse to find some coins.

206

'Um, I'll get it, since you paid for my fine and all.' John was sniggering now.

As soon as she handed him the video box and ice-cream I legged it out the shop as fast as my legs could take me.

'What was that all about? Wet pussy? I'll give you a..' He was laughing uncontrollably.

'DON'T even go there.' I snapped.

'Ah but you always seem to like it…'

'No John. Seriously. If you knew who rented that film you wouldn't be comparing it to our sex life.'

He raised an eyebrow.

'OK, OK. It was my dad. He's got my spare Apollo card. I got a load of stick from some annoying lads in the shop when that bitch of a sales assistant loudly announced that I owed money for 9 Lives of a Wet Pussy and then there was talk of Free Willy and then…'

He was doubled over laughing. And then I couldn't help myself. We fell into each other giggling relentlessly, until tears were leaking from our eyes.

We composed ourselves and headed back to John's. I'd already dropped Trevor off there so we had the whole family under one roof, Pulp Fiction and a tub of luxury Bailey's flavoured ice-cream.

Everything was perfect until…

'We're going to have to think about finding homes for our pups aren't we?'

'Oh John, no I can't even think about that.'

'Well, we can't very well look after five dogs between us?'

'I know. But I'm getting quite attached. Especially to that little one.'

I pointed at the little wriggler we had named Daffy.

'I know!' I exclaimed. 'I'll ask me dad. He loves Trev, well, most of the time, and he's a bit lonely. He could do with a new project. A reason to get out on a daily walk.'

'Thought your dad was more into pussy.'

I put my fingers down my throat to demonstrate my

disgust at the imagery he'd just allowed to re-enter my mind.

'Come on, let's watch the film. There's a dance scene we need to re-enact.'

'You've seen it!' I said mock-accusingly.

'Aye. But it's a good 'un.'

When I woke up the next day, I crept into the hallway to call the counselling service. John wasn't in work until later so he was having a lie in.

I dialled the number, it was an answer machine, so I left a message.

'Hi, um. It's Emma Barclay. Someone left me a message yesterday about a counselling appointment for Wednesday. I'd like to take that please. I'll be there for 10:40. Thanks.' I put the phone down.

'You're having counselling?' John appeared behind me. I hadn't even heard him get up.

'Oh. Yes. Nothing to worry about though. All the Americans do it.'

'Anything you want to chat about? I mean…if it helps?'

'I don't really know. I don't really know why I'm going. I've no idea what I'll say. Maybe we can chat after? But really, don't worry – there will be no big revelations or anything.'

He just gave me a smile and kissed me on my forehead. Slowly and gently. He made me feel immediately relaxed. I wasn't embarrassed in front of him.

However, when the day of the appointment came around, I was ridiculously nervous. I couldn't cope with telling the boss why I needed to take the morning off; so I pulled a sicky. Said I had a stomach upset. No doubt there would be more syphilitic rumours going around soon.

I had no idea what we were going to talk about, me and this counsellor. This was going to be more awkward than a first date. This was going to be more awkward than the video shop shenanigans.

Was it like the agony aunt pages in More! magazine? Would I be talking about my sex life? Whether to introduce my boyfriend to Dad? How to tell if said boyfriend was cheating on me?

Would I be looking at rough diagrams of sexual positions that would help us find the G-spot and therefore, according to the magazines, strengthen our relationship?

God, teenagers have it bad reading all that crap. As if any teenager in the world has ever experienced anything more interesting than over-excitable rutting by a spotty male. Teenage sex memories. Ugh.

I had literally no idea what happened in a counselling session and yet here I was, about to find out.

It was being held in the doctor's surgery so I wandered in ten minutes early and took a seat in the waiting room, flicking through the same copy of Cosmopolitan I'd picked up last time. Once again, I felt like a bit of a fraud sitting amongst older people struggling to breathe and screaming babies with colic. Was I really just here because a priest suggested I should have a cuppa and a chat with someone?

They called my name and I wandered down the corridor, knocking softly on the door before wandering into the room and taking my seat in front of 'Belinda'.

I was offered a glass of water, which I accepted but of course never touched. Who was supposed to start? Was it like confession? Was there a line to say?

Forgive me Belinda, for my head is tormented

Maybe not.

'So tell me about why you're here, Emma.'

I had no idea where to start. So I just told the truth. I told Belinda that a priest had suggested I talked to someone, and about my strange 'fainting spells', and that I knew counsellors were people you could talk to. That I might have some inner turmoil to iron out and that turning 27 might not be the problem.

'Why did you think turning 27 might be a problem in the first place?' she asked.

I went on to explain how the death of Kurt Cobain and the idea of the 27 club terrified me. How it always seemed to happen to rock stars. How loss of innocence, rock music and fame might be the root of all evil.

Saying it all out loud like that I suddenly felt *very* stupid. And I told her that I felt a bit stupid saying it but that I still had these feelings of doom and of dread about turning 27.

'It's not stupid, Emma. You just need to figure out why you're feeling like that. It probably goes a bit deeper than you think. But because you haven't figured it out yet, because you haven't found the real answer, you're clutching at straws and none of it makes much sense.'

She said we needed to think about the themes I was worrying about and delve a bit deeper. We started with rock music and I talked about the bands I loved, and the ones we'd lost.

Given Mum and Dad always listened to rock music and seeing how their relationship ended also didn't help matters. I wondered what Mum listened to when she was fucking her bit on the side. Was she listening to the same tunes Dad was listening to whilst he was cooking my tea because she was late home? Again.

I know they say art is all about interpretation but how could the same musical art inspire such drastically different responses.

I told Belinda that I couldn't think of a single pop star who died aged 27.

'That might be because their age hasn't been the focus like it has for some of the rock stars you're talking about. If somebody playing, say, classical music died aged twenty-seven, if wouldn't have fit with the 27 club narrative, and so it wouldn't have been found beneath that headline. Could that be the case?'

Ooh she was good.

'Possibly, but it just seems so strange. And there's something about rock music. Something about how they live a life of darkness. It's appealing in some ways, but equally, it makes me feel a bit anxious.'

'When you say darkness, what do you mean?'

'Well. There's all this pain. There's all this talk of wild behaviour. Violence. Pain. Anguish. As though they've been tainted.'

'In what way could somebody be tainted? Have you been tainted, Emma?'

'Maybe. I don't know. I've had sex with people I barely know. And I've been drunk and off my face before.'

'Lots of people have. But it doesn't cause everyone to think they might die at a very specific age. Why do you think feelings of being tainted, of loss of innocence, especially concern you?'

'Because I know what it can do.'

I started to feel panicked. The idea of innocence always took me back to the halcyon days before Mum's affair. Of being very young. Never mind losing my virginity. Never mind getting drunk for the first time or watching Dallas for the first time. The only feelings of innocence I had were pre-parental-affair.

We never talked about the affair.

'When did you feel like you lost your innocence, Emma?'

'When I was eight.'

'And what happened when you were eight?'

I didn't want to go there. Not to that year. I was already teetering on the edge of those awful, chaotic feelings. That confused child wondering why Mummy wasn't coming home. Why only Daddy read bedtime stories now. Why Daddy had to make the tea, because he bought Alphabites instead of Smiley Faces and it just wasn't the same.

I was already in the moments when my world changed forever.

'Mum had an affair.'

I'd blurted it out and realised I had never really talked about it. I had a little to Dave, but never about how I felt about it. Everything I had said previously was based on the facts. Pure and simple.

God. That's a bad choice of words.

I felt a combination of relief and anger well up inside me. I continued with my outpouring, thinking maybe this was going to make me feel a bit better. 'I nagged and nagged to go to dance class. I was bored of swimming. I mean, I could swim easily by that point, and I just wanted to freestyle it. I was happier knocking about on the inflatables at the pool on a weekend than swimming length after length. So I needed something new to do. And that's where she met him. One of the parents of the other kids.' I said. 'Who I became really good friends with. We didn't have much in common. I liked Dad's Fleetwood Mac music and she liked Abba. But we always seemed to be going places together.'

'And how did it make you feel? The affair, I mean.'

'Like it was my fault. Like if I hadn't been so selfish, so desperate to be the next dancing queen, to impress my mates in the playground with scissor-kicks and side-ways splits, it wouldn't have happened.'

Belinda explained that we can't control other people's lives. We can't control how they respond to events. Only how we do. And after all, I was the child, and Mum was the adult. So now we needed to explore how I responded to my mum's affair…

I described how I had no idea it was happening and how bad that made me feel. How, thinking back, I should have seen it. I should have noticed the signs. I was the one spending so much time with Mum and her fancy man. But Belinda reminded me that I was a child at the time. I was experiencing it with the young, innocent mind of a child. Yet I was reflecting on the situation years later with the brain of an adult. I didn't have that brain when I was eight and I probably didn't know that sex and affairs even existed.

She was right. I knew she was right. But I was so angry. So angry with Mum. Dad was heartbroken. His life just seemed to go downhill. It wasn't fair that he lost his job. That he had to look after me as a single parent cos Mum had left. That he had to learn to put my hair up into a half ponytail with his thick clumsy fingers and me screaming the house down because he was pulling it too tight. That he had to have 'the talk' with me when I went on my first date down the leisure centre. That he had to buy my first Tampax and bra.

Poor Dad. He had enough on his plate dealing with the fact his wife had left him with another man. But he still carried on caring for me. He just didn't carry on caring for himself. There was never anyone else in his life. Well, until now, if Barbara Carpenter was anything to go by...

'You're obviously very angry with your mum. Have you told her this?'

'I can't.' I said.

'Why don't you feel you can speak to her, Emma?'

'Because she's dead.'

I'd said it. Out loud. I can't remember the last time I said it. I was starting to feel naked. Exposed. I didn't talk about this. We never talked about this stuff out loud. I never talked about Mum in this way.

My heart was pounding. My throat closing up. My chest heaving nervously as I desperately, desperately tried to keep it all in. To stay composed. To not go there. Not again.

'How did your mum die, Emma?'

'Car crash.' I murmured, fidgeting in my seat as I spoke, feeling like a child all over again. 'It was when we found out about the affair. We only found out when we got the phone call. She was with him.'

'So you never got to speak to your mum about what had been happening?'

'No. But it was years ago. What's this got to do with me now?

My voice was becoming stunted by my erratic breathing. 'Do you miss her, Emma?'

Being prompted to consider this, I felt angry at first. Angry that, yes, I did miss her. Angry that she made herself leave us. Angry that she wasn't there for me. As if she chose to leave me. Because I loved her and I needed her.

And with that, I broke down into tears over my mum. For the first time in years.

I really *did* miss her. So much. Before the accident, I'd never have even dreamed that my mum could be involved in a sordid affair. I didn't know what a sordid affair was. She was just my mum. The woman who made me Findus crispy pancakes with chips and peas; who always got the water sprinkler and empty Fairy liquid bottles out when Dave came round so we could have water-fights; and who always helped me choose the most thoughtful presents for Dad for Christmas (although, thinking back, she did let the Hai Karate aftershave slip through the quality control net that one time...)

We were happy. Weren't we?

But my mum seemingly had other needs. She upset the applecart. She upset the norm.

Why were all the lines becoming blurry? Why was my loving, wonderful mum cheating on my dad? Having sex in cars with another man.

I remember finding out about the affair. Sometime after the car crash. They'd both been found dead in the front of the car. At the time, I just thought they were friends. They took us to dance class. Why wouldn't they be in a car together?

Me and Abigail had been left standing at the end of class, after our best ever Bee Gees routine, and we knew something was wrong. Everyone else had gone home. The dance teacher started getting twitchy. There was no phone in the dance hall so she asked us to get changed in the changing rooms and wait a while longer. But my mum and Abigail's dad never arrived.

As the minutes ticked on, the dance teacher decided she would have to take us home. So she let us into the back seat of her car. It was covered with magazines and knackered old dance shoes, McDonalds burger boxes and the same box of paper coated tubular cardboard things Mum always had in the bathroom. It wasn't a nice clean car like ours was.

As we started to drive off I noticed that our car was still parked outside, from two hours ago. They must have gone somewhere in Abigail's car.

I didn't say anything. Nobody was in it, after all. And you just put your faith in adults at that age don't you. The dance teacher would make sure everything was OK.

We got home and Dad was watching the snooker on the telly. He looked surprised to see me. The dance teacher told him that me and my friend Abigail hadn't been picked up.

He didn't look as confused as I felt. He looked angry. And when the dance teacher left, he opened another can of lager. And another. I sat with my scratch art kit, gradually uncovering the silver outline of an owl on a branch. Barely able to look up. Sensing there was something very different and very wrong in our house today.

Snooker balls were knocking, kids were happily screaming outside and I could hear the sound of next door's radio drifting through the lounge window.

Dad had another beer.

And then the phone rang in the hall.

And my world changed forever.

Dad seemed to go into some kind of shock. He walked like a ghost back into the kitchen, poured a whiskey, necked it and then crouched down beside where I was sitting at the table. He put his big hands on my skinny little arms and looked me in the eye. I remember his voice was quivering and I felt frightened because I never saw my dad like that before. And then he said it.

'Emma. I'm so sorry, love.'

I was confused. A tear rolled down my dad's cheek. A sense of dread was building up inside my little chest. Dad wasn't meant to cry? Where was Mum? Why hadn't she picked me up. It all felt so wrong.

'Your mum's been in a car crash, Emma. She's not coming back.'

I barely had a moment to take it in, but he held me tight and started sobbing. I couldn't cry. I was too confused. What did this mean?

As a child, it was as though it never actually hit me that day. Of course it did to some degree, but it was as though each day I got a little more used to the fact. When Dad dropped me at school every day. When he made my tea every night. When he took me to dance class every weekend. I never saw Abigail there again.

I told Belinda all of this.

'That must have been really hard. How old were you when you lost your mum?'

'I was eight.'

'Gosh. And how old was your mum, Emma?'

'She was 27.'

CHAPTER 13

All this therapeutic talk was making me feel tiny. As if I was back there, eight year's old. I felt this strange feeling in my chest and my throat, like I was on the verge of tears. It was constantly there. Like a child.

I left Belinda's office and its soft furnishings and pretty plants and walked back home. The air seemed different, somehow. Like after a heavy rainfall when everything looks more real. I called Dad and asked if he fancied a video and pizza night. Said I'd bring Trev and stop over if he didn't mind. He seemed happy with that. 'But can we do curry instead?'

After a night of staring at the telly (I'd managed to pick up that Flintstones movie I was desperate to watch) and stuffing our faces with Tikka Masala, barely talking, I headed off to bed. We didn't need to talk, me and Dad. I just needed to be there with him. As his daughter. I just needed to be at home and feel good about it. As if this was just normal family life.

It *was* normal family life.

The following day I was awoken by the sound of the kettle boiling and Radio 2 drifting gently up to my bedroom – a signal that it was time to get up. Light was flooding through the curtains meaning I'd slept in. The mornings had got much darker since summer said it's goodbyes and the pretty blue flowers had dropped from the lilac plant, leaving a dark and shadowy green shrub watching over the garden.

It was usually Trev that woke me in a morning, nutting my nose with his snotty beak, begging for biscuits and a walk. But he was still curled up at the bottom of my bed snoozing.

He'd barely left my side since yesterday.

I forced myself out of bed, lazily shuffled over to my dressing table in my pyjamas and checked my face in the mirror. My eyes looked puffy. They weren't used to so many tears. And a fair few fell out of them yesterday. There was no way I was going into work today. I'd have to call in sick.

Everything in that room was the same as it was almost a decade ago when I left for university. My posters were still on the wall – Prince, Madonna and The Doors. An eclectic mix, betraying my teenage confusion. And my floral bedspread was still on the bed. I remember Dad buying that for me when I wanted to be more grown-up. Victoria Plum would no longer do.

I stretched and yawned and Trevor started to sit up, almost mimicking me, looking more alert and ready for the day.

I found it comforting that Dad still listened to the same radio station in a morning with his cup of tea – which was always a strong 'builder's brew'. But even a builder would have trouble knocking that stewed beverage back. I think Dad always loved strong food and drink so much because it took away the stench of the sea that he struggled to shake off after a day of hard graft at the fish factory.

At least redundancy brought some benefits with it. He stuck with the builder's brew though. Acquired taste, I guess.

I heard 'Amadeus' playing as I trundled down the stairs, Trevor in hot pursuit wagging his tail.

'Morning Dad.'

'Oh, morning love. Kettle's on.'

He was looking highly embarrassed as his startled body movement tried to disguise the fact that I'd just caught him dancing while washing last night's dirty dishes at the sink. The Fairy liquid bubbles had gone bright yellow because of the turmeric in the curry we'd eaten.

My dad. Dancing. Who knew? Throws a great backwards power punch in those marigold gloves too.

'What you up to today, love?'

'I'll be taking Trev for a walk first if you fancy it. Then I'm seeing John later so I'll head home after the walk to get myself smartened up.'

'Dave seems to like him. Good sign.'

'Yeah' I said. I was stalling, pouring myself a cup of tea and trying to think of the best way to brooch the subject. To ask about Mum. A subject we'd never properly discussed as adults. Perhaps I'd save it for the walk.

'So when does your old man get to meet the new love of your life then?'

'You can talk!'

'What's that supposed to mean?'

'I bumped into Barbara Carpenter the other day…I've been waiting for you to tell me…'

'Oh that. Oh no. That's nothing serious.' He looked almost embarrassed. 'John on the other hand…Dave said you were really relaxed with each other. He said it was lovely.'

'He's got a big mouth.' I said. Smiling.

'So has Barbara Carpenter.' Dad added. And winked at me.

I didn't need to know the details. I was his daughter. And he was happy. He hadn't been with anyone since Mum as far as I knew. On his own for literally years. And he and Mum were together since they were in their teens. He deserved a bit of fun. Even if it was with Barbara Carpenter. Even if it was, you know, less about trips to the movies and more about trips to her bedroom. I shuddered to think. Must move on.

I pulled on a pair of jeans and my boots, wrapped a great big purple crochet scarf around my neck, threw on my black velvet coat and we headed out with Trev. Dad drove us to the coast again so we could 'enjoy the sea air'.

We pulled up into the gravelly car park, hearing the stones crunching beneath the tyres. I opened the door and Trev jumped straight out, tongue hanging out his mouth as he almost doubled back on himself galloping towards the sea whilst looking back at me in excitement. Walks never got boring for Trev. It was time *I* found more excitement in natural pursuits.

We crossed the spiky sand dunes and hit the beach. The tide wasn't too far out and the sand was slurping beneath our feet. I knew that my boots would be kicking up a sloppy trail of wet muddy sand that would spatter the back of my jeans. But I gave into it and enjoyed the walk regardless. My previous conversation with Dave started ringing in my ears. I felt so relieved that we weren't here to scatter his ashes like he'd suggested. We were, however, here to uncover our true feelings about Mum.

There was so much I needed to ask Dad, about Mum, but I had no idea how to start the conversation. We just never spoke about it. So maybe that was the best way to start...

'Why have we never really spoken about Mum, Dad?'

'We do. I'm always talking about her lilac and her Yorkshire puddings.'

'No, I mean *really* talked. We've never talked about what happened.'

He looked uncomfortable at first and carried on walking, his step quickening as if to run away from the conversation. Oh God, had I upset him?

I stopped, wondering what to do. Should I give him space? Should I even be forcing him to talk about it? But then he turned around and came back, looked me in the eye, and just started talking. About how he didn't want to burden me with the sordid details. How I was so young and then, as I got older, so much time had passed that it didn't seem right. Not to rock the boat when we were doing OK, just the two of us. And Dave, of course.

'Don't you feel like you want to talk about it? Like, getting it all out might be good.' I asked.

'Ah I'm alright Emma. I'm not the 'talking' kind of bloke. All that feelings stuff. I know I've had my moments and I've become a grumpy old bugger. But it all died inside of me years ago, to be honest. And I'm doing much better now. Honestly. But I'm happy for you to talk to me, if it helps though?'

I think he'd just been so used to not talking, he'd somehow worked it out of his system some other way. Maybe it was work. Or KP peanuts that helped him through.

'Well. I guess I just wondered why? It sounds so naïve now I'm an adult. But why did she do it? I used to think she was this wonderful, amazing person. And then she did that.'

'She *was* a wonderful amazing person. That's why it was so hard. And why I was so angry at the start. She wasn't a bad person, Emma. She just got bored. She's a human being. And we were both so young when we got together, when we had you.'

'I know. I can't imagine being a mum now, never mind at 19.'

'Yeah. We were young. We loved you. You coming along was a gift from the heavens! Well, until you fell in that slurry pit. But yeah, we tried to live like a pair of young'uns and a pair of adults at the same time. It wasn't easy. But we didn't regret it.'

'So why did she do it?'

'She was just young. That's all. She hadn't hit thirty. She told me she was struggling and I just kind of took it for granted. I knew she needed more in her life. I had just become…lazy. It's not always black and white. I didn't see it back then. But I can see it now. I don't hate her, Emma. I miss her.'

'I do too.' I said. And I started to cry. Again. What the fuck was all this about? All this crying?

Dad grabbed hold of me and gave me a big bear hug on the sand. And the blubbing intensified. Great, big, heaving tears and jolts of sadness. Things I'd never experienced before. But there were jolts of warmth and gratitude too.

We stood for a while. My nose was getting snotty and I had no tissues on me. The coastal breeze was blowing my long hair into my face and it was sticking to my nose. Trev had run over and was weaving in and around our feet. Desperately wanting a part of the family cuddle action.

Dad released me from his bear hug, put his arm round me and led me and our Trev back to the car.

Trev jumped in the back, I sat in the front, and we set off across the crunchy gravel, out of the car park and back home. And I slept like a baby for the next half hour, all the way to Dad's.

I popped back into Dad's to grab my stuff and the Flintstones video – I didn't want another fine – and this could be almost as embarrassing as being fined for porn. I kissed Dad goodbye and me and Trev dawdled back home. Trev was on his lead as we made our way through the ten-foot alley and back onto the busy shopping street, with cars taking up as much pavement as they did road, double parking to ensure everyone was within at least 100m of their own home. It was coming up to winter after all.

The video shop was shut, thankfully, so I popped the Flintstones tape in the drop-off box in the wall. We then took a left up my street and noticed that the leaves had all but dropped at last. The beautiful orange and gold colours had created a carpet of mulch on the ground and left brittle twigs looking angry and naked against the sky. But it wasn't signalling death. It was simply marking a change. And a change is as good as a rest, as they say.

I felt strangely calm. Almost as though years of pent up anger had begun to dissipate. It was slowly releasing the pressure - I'd turned the tap on and let it start seeping out. Life wasn't black and white and remembering the good bits about my mum didn't mean I was being disloyal to Dad. I could stop denying her love now. It felt almost strange to think so freely about her and at one point I found myself smiling as I remembered how she was pulling a feather boa around my neck and sending me off to Brownies as her little Janis.

I gave Trev his fresh chicken and water for tea and pulled out a chair from the kitchen table. I stood it in front of the book shelf, climbed up and pulled down the dusty box from the top. My little box of nostalgia, wrapped in Christmas wrapping to hide the crisp packets the naked box had been advertising before we rescued it from Kwik Save.

It had been years since I looked in that box. I couldn't ever let it go but, equally, I found it too hard to enjoy, so it just sat there, gathering dust. I lifted the top off the box and found photos, old club flyers, swimming badges, certificates and letters me and Dave wrote to each other as kids. I'd love to say they were meaningful letters but in fact they were just our consequences games. We'd start off a story, fold it up to cover the paragraph, then swap the pieces of paper at school, continuing the story until it reached a conclusion. It usually involved random events like Orville the Duck shagging Mrs Hillier from the library and telling her he wanted an egg sandwich before turning into Clarke Kent and running off with Margaret Thatcher.

I found some old photos of us all too. Back from the late 80s, when we were in our late teens. Me, trying to make my face look haunted with the pout of Black Cherry lipstick, which was fighting for the limelight against a high volume, highly misjudged spiral perm I was, at that point, desperately trying to grow out. And there was Dave with his ripped jeans, Morrissey haircut and a face full of gentle attitude. We looked as though life was serious shit and we were ready to dwell in it.

I delved a bit deeper, flicking through the photos of me and Dad in Grimsby eating chips after we'd been to the old jailhouse. I remembered my dad slagging off the fish saying it was nowt compared to what we landed in Hull. And then I found a pic of me and Dave at Hull Fair learning how to smoke having nicked a packet of ciggies from his next-door neighbour. We were soaking wet from riding the log flume over and over again – my favourite fairground ride. We both looked ridiculous, shame the cigarette smoking became second nature not long after that.

I kept rifling through the box, almost with an urgency to re-discover mine and Mum's relationship. And there they were at the bottom of the pile. The photos of me in my bell-bottomed dance costume, Mum squeezing me tight as I held up my little dance trophy. She looked so proud and I got that weird sense of achiness in my chest - the kind that feels so sad and torturous but yet so comforting and indulgent. I started to realise it was genuine. I started to realise I could still love her.

I pulled one of the picture frames off the mantelpiece containing some random arty postcard and replaced it with the photo. Why shouldn't I enjoy the dancing? Why shouldn't I enjoy her cuddles and pride. Yes, around that time, she was cheating on Dad. I was angry about that. But there's always something terrible happening somewhere in the world when you're enjoying yourself. You can't control that.

A warm feeling spread across my chest. Something I hadn't felt for such a long time. It was as though I could finally be happy without placing restrictions on it. I didn't have to taint it with thoughts of *'yes, but, Mum's affair, Dave's cancer, Dad's depression, your imminent doom'*. I could just feel it. It felt so freeing and, more than anything, like a huge relief. Like so much angst had suddenly vanished.

I sat on the sofa in silence for a few moments, looking over at the framed photo of Mum, Trevor on my lap. I could hear him breathing peacefully, and I watched his rib cage moving up and down in a reassuringly consistent routine. We were both healthy and happy beings – even if his doggy IBS still had its occasional flare up.

I realised that I hadn't enjoyed silence for so many years. I was always trying to drown it out, replace it with something distracting. I let out an audible sigh of contentedness. And I had lots to look forward to tonight as well.

I'd invited John over to the Angel again. It was *our* local now, and it was the perfect pre-Oasis meeting place. He seemed as much a part of the furniture as Doreen was. Thankfully, she was still propping up the bar – still going strong was our Doreen.

John walked in, waved at Brenda and Bob, responded to Dave's '*want a drink*' action with a '*yes please*' action and then took a pew and kissed me.

Dave returned with the drinks and we were just getting comfy, talking about our top five gigs of all time, when Dad walked in. Well, now was as good a time as ever, I guessed.

I leant over to John and whispered 'that's me Dad over there.'

He looked ever so slightly nervous, but smiled warmly. 'Hope he likes me' he whispered whilst squeezing my hand. To be fair, on meeting your girlfriend's dad for the first time, especially when it's sprung on you, if there isn't a slight degree of nervousness, you'd have to be a narcissist surely? Dads are so important. At least to me, anyway.

'Dave.' Dad said.

'Tel.' Dave said.

'And you must be the bloke keeping our Emma on her toes.' Dad said to John, holding out his hand.

'Aye. Good to meet you. I've heard lots about you.'

'Same here. Mainly from this one.' Dad nodded at Dave before turning his attention back to John. 'Our Emma tends to keep things of the romantic nature close to her chest where her dad's concerned. No need to worry though, it's all good.'

'Thank God for that.' John said as he picked up his pint and took a well-deserved sip to calm his nerves.

Dad gave me a wink. What is it with men and winking? 'So, you're all off to see this Oasis band tonight then?'

'At least the Adelphi'll let 'em in wearing their shoddy footwear.' Brenda mocked, listening in from the bar.

Doreen added: 'No class that place.' Had she been? Had Doreen rocked out in The Adelphi? Maybe she went with Father William. Two old rockers living it up.

We'd all got tickets for Oasis. I'd bought a pair for me and Dave when I made us go to LA's. What on earth was I thinking back then. And Dave had bought a ticket anyway just to be sure. Apparently I was far too 'relaxed' about getting it sorted. And Dave said it could well spell the end of our friendship if I messed up on the tickets so really, he was safeguarding our relationship.

It was Dave's idea to offer the spare one to John. This was true acceptance. This proved that John was certainly *not* a cunt.

We had a good hour until we needed to leave. It was only a five-minute walk. So we got another drink in with Dad. With a Drambuie chaser.

Dad asked John all about Newcastle. All about his family. Where he grew up, etc. He was seemingly impressed with John's equally working-class, socialist roots. And it didn't take long until tales from Question Time cropped up.

Dad discovered that John's parents had him when they were really young, too. 'Me and Emma's mum were young when we had her.' Dad said. 'I remember we were actually supposed to be travelling up to Newcastle to see the Stones at the City Hall back in the 70s. But the babysitter cancelled on us and we missed it. Gutted. But I wouldn't swap this one.'

Dad squeezed my chin between his thumb and finger as if I were six again. I blushed a little, feeling vulnerable and small in front of John, but I loved my dad's fatherly affection all the same. Until he took a swig of his bitter and asked loudly:

'So how's the old knacker then Dave?'

'Dad!'

'S'what he says.' Dad defended his rather abrupt choice of language.

'Yeah. It's looking good. No need for radiotherapy. They reckon they got it in good time. I'll be here til I'm old like you, Tel.'

'Good to hear.' Dad said and winked at him.

'Right, come on Dave, let's get the round in and give these two five minutes.'

Off they went. For all the seemingly straight-talking, no messing cancer banter, I saw Dad put his arm round Dave as they headed to the bar. I love that I can share my dad.

John leant over the table, leaning in to me.

'Our Emma.' He said, mimicking my dad. I giggled, 'your birthday's coming up isn't it?'

'It is, yep.' I said, no longer panicking about doom or death. Just wondering what kind of card John would get me. Would it be one of those contemporary Athena style cards? Or would he get one with a bunch of flowers on the front, foil writing and a rubbish poem inside? I wasn't too confident, especially given his home furnishings left a lot to be desired. But then he was a good cook. And he must have good taste, he picked me after all! That's what my Dad would have said anyway.

'So, I've taken the liberty and booked you a birthday treat.' He said.

He's booked a birthday treat? Booked? That's not a material gift. That means he wants to spend time with me. That means a romantic weekend city break. Maybe we'll head to Edinburgh? Barcelona? Maybe a cottage in the Moors? We could be like Cathy and Heathcliff!

'John. You really needn't have.' I said, being falsely coy. 'But I'm glad you did.' I joined in with the winking.

'Good.' He said. 'Make sure you book these dates off work. We'll be taking Trev and Dixie too. As well as any of our little pups who might be left behind.'

He handed me a copy of the booking form to check over the dates. It was for the weekend just after my birthday.

Four days in a caravan park in Withernsea.

ACKNOWLEDGEMENTS

This book has been written and produced with the help and patience of so many who have endured my relentless impatience. My wonderful agent, Jo; my long-suffering husband Chris ("will you just read this edited passage again please"); my stepson, Sam ("Gen Z love the 90's right?") my friends and family (Mum, Julia and Jayne who are forced to read everything I write) and my dad who inspired my love of writing and music. Special thanks also to Kirk Teasdale, a designer who totally and truly gets it; Paul 'Gigsy' McGivern for sharing stories of life on the road; Angela Clarke for her early read and encouragement; Caroline Goldsmith for adding a professional touch; Sam Missingham for expert advice; and Live Theatre and Arts Council England for believing in the concept.

THANKS

Thank you to everyone who contributed a piece of their youth to the design process!

Bethany Clift
Simon Crook
Jane Davis
Matthew Evans
Rowan Horner
Paul 'Gigsy' McGivern
Sarah Mole
Catherine Murphy
Martyn Nancarrow
Dave Nellist
Victoria Page
Kerry Ramsay
Julie Rea
Simon Reed-Linton

And special thanks to our whippet cover model, He-Man, and his dads, Paul Taylor and Christopher Mitton for the photo

ABOUT THE AUTHOR

Lucy is a writer, mental health campaigner and PR consultant whose work has appeared in The Independent, The I Paper, NME, Red Magazine, Den of Geek, Huff Post and many more. She is also a former columnist with Sarah Millican's Standard Issue magazine and often interviews guests for the Standard Issue podcast. She is passionate about challenging mental health and particularly addiction stigma, has worked with the media in PR and marketing for over 18 years and has experienced anxiety for even longer. Lucy works closely with recovery charities, volunteering her time to campaign and support people living with all kinds of addictions.

Her first book, A Series of Unfortunate Stereotypes, was released by Trigger in 2018.

Follow Lucy on:

Twitter: @lucyenichol

Instagram: lucyenichol

Facebook: Lucy Nichol Author

Sign up for Lucy's newsletter: lucynichol.substack.com

Printed in Great Britain
by Amazon

77177189R00138